Healthy GUT, *Happy* YOU

Dr Emma Short

The Healthy Happy
Gut Doctor

The Book Guild Ltd

First published in Great Britain in 2024 by
The Book Guild Ltd
Unit E2 Airfield Business Park,
Harrison Road, Market Harborough,
Leicestershire. LE16 7UL
Tel: 0116 2792299
www.bookguild.co.uk
Email: info@bookguild.co.uk
X: @bookguild

Typeset in 11pt Minion Pro

Printed on FSC accredited paper
Printed and bound in Great Britain by 4edge Limited

ISBN 978 1835740 163

British Library Cataloguing in Publication Data.
A catalogue record for this book is available from the British Library.

Contents

Introduction

Towards the end of 2022, I was feeling out of kilter. It was as though my sparkle had been snuffed out. I woke up one day and realised that I hadn't worn lipstick for months and I couldn't remember when I'd last laughed. I wasn't depressed, but it seemed as though all of my energy had been drained away.

I knew my stress levels were unhealthily high – I'd started a new job that, although I loved, was really busy, with an hour commute in both directions, and I was training for a marathon that my heart wasn't committed to. My beloved grandad had sadly passed away, which left our family heartbroken. On top of all this, we had been having our kitchen renovated. There had been mishap after mishap, meaning that we'd been living in chaos and eating rubbish for months. My usually healthy diet had deteriorated into takeaways, ultra-processed 'treats', a lack of wholefoods and late-night snacking.

I started to experience episodes of palpitations, which I've suffered from before, and I know they're my body's way of telling me to slow down. I occasionally woke at night with chest pains – my food pipe would go into spasm, which is something that happens when I'm not eating properly. One of the worst things was that my patience was at its end, and my capacity to cope with life's ups and downs was exhausted. I knew I didn't want to carry on feeling this way and that I needed to get my well-being back on track.

I have always been fascinated by the gut microbiome and will happily spend hours reading the latest research studies which explore this area. I believe the gut microbiome has the potential to have a major impact on the way we practise medicine in the future, in terms of health promotion, disease prediction, disease prevention and disease management.

I knew that if I wanted to feel like the old me again, if I wanted to feel happy and energised, one of the things I needed to do was to take greater care of the trillions of bacteria living in my intestines. I needed to provide them with better fuels, so that they could do their job of looking after me. But nurturing the incredible ecosystem within our guts doesn't just mean feeding them well. In the same way that we need to have a holistic approach to improving the well-being of ourselves, we need to do the same with the bugs in our gut. We need to think about how our activity levels, sleeping patterns, stress and even our relationships impact their ability to thrive.

I started by changing my diet to one which was 'gut healthy', and my spirits lifted within days. Two weeks later, I was a different person – I was sleeping better, I had stopped craving sweet snacks and my mood was back to normal.

This book is a guide to the mind-blowing community of microbes which live inside us. I hope that it will provide you with the knowledge you need so that you, too, can make tweaks to your lifestyle that will help your gut bacteria to flourish. This will, in turn, help you to feel happier and healthier. I'll look at what the gut microbiome is, what it does and how a variety of lifestyle factors affect its composition. At the end of the book, I've included my favourite gut-healthy recipes, which are simple and quick to prepare, and which taste delicious.

Dr Emma Short
@dr_emmashort
The Healthy Happy Gut Doctor

What is the Gut Microbiome?

Our gut microbiome is utterly amazing! It's only been over the last one to three decades that we've really come to have a greater understanding of what it does, and the role it plays in health and disease. A *microbiome* describes the collection of microorganisms which live in a certain environment. Specifically, it refers to their genetic material, and we should strictly use the term *microbiota*, but I'll use both of these throughout this book.

Microorganisms are tiny creatures that are too small to be seen with our eyes – we would need a microscope to see them. A microbiome can include bacteria, viruses, protozoa, fungi and archaea. As humans, we have many different microbial ecosystems that live on us, within us and around us. Can you believe that as you're sitting here reading this book, you're even surrounded by your own unique microbial cloud, which is largely derived from your skin, mouth and throat bacteria!

We have microbiomes living in a variety of different anatomical and physiological niches–for example, on our skin, in our airways and in our genital tracts. The gut microbiome refers to the microorganisms which live in our gastrointestinal tract, the tube which extends from our mouth through to our anus, including our oesophagus/gullet, stomach, small intestine and large intestine. It's the most diverse of our microbiomes and the largest numerically. Some of the bacteria inside us are there purely for their own benefit (the selfish commensals – they take from us what they need to grow), some live in us and we both benefit (symbiotic species) and others can potentially cause diseases (pathogenic bacteria).

Most of the research into the gut microbiome has focussed on the bacteria which are found in the large bowel (colon). There are around thirty-nine trillion bacteria present in our gut, which is similar to the number of human cells we're made from. For every human gene we have, there are at least one hundred bacterial genes, and the gut microbiome can weigh up to a tremendous 2kg, so accounts for a not-insignificant part of our body mass.

Within any individual, there are usually between two hundred and five hundred different bacterial species, but the total number of potential species is greater than a thousand. The composition of the gut microbiome varies throughout the length of the gastrointestinal tract, depending on the physical and chemical environment and the fuels which are available to the bacteria. For example, the stomach, with its acidic pH, abundance of digestive enzymes and frequent churning movements, is a harsh place for microorganisms to try and set up home. Instead, they opt for the large bowel, which is a much calmer place to live.

Generally, the further you travel along the gut, the greater the diversity of species and the greater the number of organisms present. The composition is unique to each individual, but the major bacteria present in the Western world tend to be members of the *Bacteroidetes* and *Firmicutes* families.

The composition of our microbiome varies throughout the course of our lives. It is thought that between 50 and 70% is a relatively static, core community, and the remaining component is a variable community that changes largely according to environmental factors, including our diet. We'll take a deeper dive into these environmental factors throughout this book.

Dysbiosis

A term that you might have heard in the context of the gut microbiome is *dysbiosis*. This describes an imbalance in gut microbiota that can have a negative impact on the person that they're living in. It usually refers to a reduction in microbial diversity, so that fewer species are present, but it can also mean an imbalance between the 'good' and 'harmful' species.

What does the gut microbiome do?

The gut microbiome is vital for our health and well-being. It has a huge range of functions, many of which we're only just beginning to understand. Some of its most important roles are:

· Defence

Our gut lining is incredible – we have an 'intestinal barrier' between the contents of our bowel and the insides of our bodies. This barrier must be permeable, or 'leaky', enough to allow nutrients and water to be absorbed, but it must also keep out potentially dangerous bacteria or other substances that we might ingest. Our gut microbiome, along with a layer of mucus and the specialised epithelial cells that line our intestines, is a key part of this barrier.

The gut microbiome acts as an army of bouncers, protecting us against unwanted visitors. By taking up space in our guts, our gut bacteria form a physical barrier which helps to stop invading species from being able to cause mischief. Our gut bacteria also use the fuel sources in our intestines for their own growth, so that less fuel is available to invading species. Some of our healthy bacteria are even able to produce antibiotic-like molecules, and they play a role in the production and composition of the mucus barrier.

· Immune System

Our immune system is an intricate collection of organs, cells, proteins and chemical messengers. Its major function is to protect us from infections, but some of our immune cells patrol our bodies looking out for tumours, which they may attack. Our immune system is divided into two parts: the innate and adaptive systems. The innate immune system provides 'non-specific' protection, whereas the adaptive immune system is designed to recognise and attack specific targets. If we think of our immune system as being an army, and our bodies as being a castle, the innate component would keep out *all* intruders, whereas the adaptive immune system might shoot at attacking soldiers, but only if they were wearing a specific type of helmet. Different immune cells are involved in the different immune responses, but the vast majority of our immune cells, a huge 70–80%, are found in our gut.

Inflammation is part of the immune system's response to a harmful stimulus, such as an infection or an injury. For example, if we cut our skin, the area around the wound becomes red, warm, swollen and tender. This happens because our blood vessels dilate to deliver inflammatory cells and chemical messengers to the site of injury in order to start the repair and healing process. In this context, the inflammatory process is said to be 'acute' as it occurs in response to a specific event and it only lasts for a short time period. 'Chronic inflammation' describes inflammation which lasts longer, from weeks to months to years. Different inflammatory cells and different chemical messengers are involved, and the inflammation can occur throughout the body. Chronic inflammation is associated with a variety of diseases, including diabetes, heart disease, cancer and Alzheimer's.

Our immune system protects us from potential dangers, but for some people, it can cause significant problems. For example, if their immune cells start to mount an attack against their own organs. These 'autoimmune diseases' include type 1 diabetes, rheumatoid arthritis and lupus.

The gut microbiome is involved in the development, maintenance and activity of both our innate and adaptive immune systems, and in regulating levels of inflammation. Some of its major roles are to help white blood cells to mature so that they can produce antibodies or fight viruses, to suppress inappropriate inflammation, to help to make cells 'immune tolerant' so they don't attack our own bodies and to modulate the activity of 'antigen-presenting cells', which are involved in boosting our immune response.

It's therefore not surprising that gut dysbiosis is associated with inappropriate immune and inflammatory responses, not just in our bowel, but also in other organs. For example, studies have shown that the microbiome of a baby's first poo, and their gut microbiome at the age of one month, is significantly different between healthy babies and those who go on to develop asthma and allergies. The effects are thought to be partially mediated by a product of the microbiome 12, 13-diHOME, which has pro-inflammatory effects, which may impair immune tolerance, and which reduces the numbers of cells that can regulate and suppress the activity of other immune cells.

· Synthetic Function, Metabolism and Harvesting Energy from Food
Our gut bacteria have an important synthetic function – they can produce vitamins, including some of the B vitamins and vitamin K, along with amino acids, which are the building blocks for making proteins. They can also synthesise neurotransmitters, which are chemical messengers that allow nerves to communicate with each other. These include serotonin, dopamine, GABA and noradrenaline. Some of these chemicals are involved in mental health conditions, but when they are produced in the gut, they do not pass directly into the brain. Instead they can have an effect through their activity on local nerves.

One of the major roles of the microbiome is in the fermentation of non-digestible carbohydrates to produce short-chain fatty acids (SCFAs). Non-digestible carbohydrates are known as 'fibre' and they include resistant starches, cellulose and pectin.

The major SCFAs are acetate, propionate and butyrate. These are produced in a ratio of 60:20:20, with acetate being the most abundant. Most production by our bacteria occurs in the large bowel and most are absorbed rather than lost in our poo. The SCFAs have a vast range of effects throughout our bodies, including maintenance of the intestinal barrier, acting as a fuel for the cells that line our intestines and protecting against the development of bowel cancer. SCFAs also modulate the growth and development of nervous tissue, affect communication between nerves and are involved in the maintenance of our blood-brain barrier (BBB). The BBB is a highly specialised system of blood vessels that protects our brains from toxic substances in the blood, but which still allows nutrients to enter.

SCFAs are also important in regulating appetite, in the control of cholesterol levels and in the metabolism of sugars and fats. Importantly, they can have anti-inflammatory effects both in the gut and throughout the body, and they can regulate oxygen levels in the gut, which helps to prevent dysbiosis.

· The Gut-Brain Axis

The gut-brain axis describes the two-way communication between our intestines and our brains. Our brain talks to our gut and our guts talk back. Communication occurs through nerves, hormones, our immune system and the metabolic products of our gut bacteria, including SCFAs. Through these routes of communication, our gut microbiome can impact our mood, stress responses and cognitive functions such as learning and memory.

How Do We Assess the Microbiome?

To assess someone's microbiome, we typically examine their poo and the bacteria which are in it! Traditionally, the process involved trying to grow bacteria in the laboratory, but this took a lot of time and hard work, and it wasn't always successful as some species have very strict growth requirements, so didn't always survive outside of the gut. It's thought that we understood less than 1% of the gut microbiome using this technique.

Over recent years, genomic technologies have become more accessible. 'Next generation sequencing' techniques involve extracting genetic material from the bacteria, then amplifying and examining it. There are two methods commonly used – one looks at a single specific gene (*16S rRNA*), and the details of the gene allow us to know which species are present and in what quantity. The second technique examines *all* of the bacterial genes, so we can appreciate not just which species are there, but also what their functions are likely to be. If we want to dive even deeper, we can look at which genes are active, or which proteins and chemicals are being made by the bacteria, although these techniques aren't currently used as often.

At the moment, gut microbiome testing isn't performed in the NHS, as there isn't enough evidence to translate many of the research findings into the clinical setting, and there aren't standardised methods of microbiome analysis. It is carried out as part of research projects and commercially. In the future, it may have the potential to predict the risk of developing certain diseases, to diagnose specific diseases and to predict someone's response to treatment. However, presently, microbiome analysis can give a general indication of someone's health, but it must be taken in the context of the whole person, including their genetics, their lifestyle, any health problems, any medications they take and any other health-related biomarkers/measurements.

What Factors Affect the Composition of the Microbiome?

For our health, it's beneficial to have a highly diverse gut microbiome. It's thought that we are generally germ-free when we are babes in the womb, and we rapidly acquire our microbiome as we are born. Babies initially have low bacterial diversity, but their gut microbiome significantly matures over the first two years of life, and it is relatively stable by the age of three years.

Our gut microbiome exhibits a 'founder effect' – this means that the initial bacteria which colonise the gut act as bosses, controlling which subsequent species are allowed to move in.

The first major factor which affects the composition of the microbiome is the mode of delivery – either via the vaginal canal or by caesarean section. Babies born by caesarean have a different composition of their microbiome, with different species present, but this effect is diminished by the time of their first birthday. Generally, babies born vaginally have higher numbers of species that are found in the maternal vagina and gut, whereas babies born by caesarean have more skin-type organisms. It's also important to consider that babies born by caesarean may have had a medical reason for this, and this in itself could potentially impact the microbiome. The babies may have received medications such as antibiotics, and this will delay the maturation of the microbiome.

The next factor is the method of feeding – whether the baby receives breast milk or bottle milk. Breast milk really is incredible. As well as supplying nutrients to the baby, it contains complex sugar molecules that have no nutritional value for the baby but are there purely for the baby's developing microbiome. Formula feeding is associated with reduced bacterial richness. Babies who suckle from their mums come into contact with the bacteria on the nipple and surrounding skin, whereas babies who are bottle-fed encounter different species on the plastic teat.

Over the first years, there are many, many different factors that are important in determining the composition of the microbiome. These include the type of foods consumed when weaning begins, the number of siblings, any pets– especially dogs, whether the baby goes to a childcare facility, whether they live in a rural or urban environment, and even whether the dishes are hand-washed or are cleaned in the dishwasher!

The Microbiome in Disease

We've seen how important the gut microbiome is in our health, and we now understand that abnormalities in the microbiome are seen in a vast range of diseases. These include obesity, bowel cancer, diabetes, heart disease, depression, anxiety, inflammatory bowel disease and eczema. In all of these, the disease is associated with dysbiosis, specifically a *reduction in microbial diversity*. The microbiome in the disease state is a bit like a sparse desert, whereas when we are healthy, our microbiomes are similar to a beautiful country garden, rich with a vast range of different species.

Although disease is associated with dysbiosis, this doesn't necessarily mean that the dysbiosis is causing the disease. It could be a cause or it could be an effect of the disease process– for example, through changes in diet, medications or other lifestyle factors. The dysbiosis could also be a completely random finding.

In order to really understand the role that the microbiome plays in disease, we first need to establish an association, we then need to prove that the dysbiosis is causative and we then need to delve even deeper to try and understand the mechanisms for causation.

For some diseases, dysbiosis has been shown to be one potential causative factor–for example: obesity, anxiety, depression and multiple sclerosis. The studies which have shown this have often been done in germ-free mice, which are mice that have been brought up in a sterile environment. A typical experiment will involve obtaining the faeces from a patient with a specific disease, transplanting this into the mice, then observing the mice to see whether they develop the disease in question.

· Obesity

We have some understanding about how dysbiosis can cause obesity. Individuals with obesity have around 7.5% less bacterial diversity than people who are not overweight, and they often have a change in the ratio of *Bacteroides* and *Firmicutes* species. A 20% increase in *Firmicutes* species is associated with extracting an additional 150 kilocalories every day from our meals. Over the days, weeks and months, this adds up to huge amount of surplus energy. It is hard to believe that two people could eat absolutely identical meals, but one person will take on board fewer calories than another! The gut microbiome in people with obesity is associated with increased hunger and enhanced food intake, increased uptake of triglycerides (a type of fat) into fat cells and reduced energy expenditure.

In obesity, there may be increased intestinal permeability to bacterial products known as lipopolysaccharides (LPS). When these get into our bodies, they can aggravate low-grade inflammation and insulin resistance, which can be a feature of obesity. Interestingly, people with obesity have lower levels of an 'anti-fat' bacteria, *Christensella*, which has been shown to reduce weight gain. Although further work needs to be done in order to fully understand how *Christensella* helps to keep people slim, it may be through modulating how much energy we burn.

Other Diseases

With many other diseases, the exact ways through which dysbiosis can have a causative effect are not certain. It could be through effects on inflammation and immunity, changes in the levels of gene expression (i.e. determining which genes are turned on or off), alterations in the levels of chemicals in the bloodstream and effects on our nervous system. Although the situation is very complicated, I've included a few examples below:

- Butyrate, one of the SCFAs, has anti-inflammatory effects.
- Butyrate reduces the risk of bowel cancer, and one of the ways it does this is by turning on genes that cause cancer cells to 'commit suicide'.
- Some gut bacteria can produce a chemical called succinate. This chemical can modulate intestinal inflammation, and levels are high in inflammatory bowel disease.
- Studies in mice have found that certain toxins produced by bacteria can reduce the activity of immune cells that are involved in fighting cancer cells. On the other hand, some of our healthy bacteria produce molecules that will actually recruit the immune cells which can attack tumours.
- Some components of our diet are metabolised by some gut bacteria to products which may increase the risk of heart attacks and stroke.

There are many potential ways in which the microbiome may be involved in causing some diseases, but additional research is required to further unpick the situation and to further increase our understanding of this very complex area.

Nutrition

Once the microbiome reaches maturity, the most important factor which impacts its composition is our diet, although several other lifestyle factors play a role. These include antibiotics and other medications, infectious diseases, especially of the gut, alcohol, smoking, exercise, sleep, social connections and timing of eating.

Fibre and Diversity

When we think about diet, the best things for our microbiome are *fibre* and *diversity* – eating as many different plant-based products as possible. This includes fruits, vegetables, nuts, legumes, herbs, spices and wholegrains.

When we're talking about fibre, we mean foods with a complex polysaccharide structure which can't be broken down by the human digestive system, as we lack the enzymes to do so. Fibres are grouped according to their viscosity (how sticky they are), solubility (whether they dissolve) and their fermentability. They generally have a structural function in plants, or they may have a storage role. It's recommended that we eat at least 30g of fibre a day, but very few people in the Western world manage this.

Many studies have shown that human populations with a diet high in complex carbohydrates, such as the Hadza hunter-gatherers from Tanzania, have high diversity of the gut microbiota. In the Western world, where we're eating much less fibre, we have around 40% less gut bacterial diversity. Generally, high-fibre diets are associated with improvements in metabolic parameters such as cholesterol levels, blood lipid levels, blood glucose levels and insulin sensitivity, and it is believed that the gut microbiome plays an important role in this.

When diets are low in fibre, microbes will switch to energetically less favourable sources for growth such as amino acids or dietary fats, resulting in a change in their metabolic output. For example, protein fermentation can give rise to branched-chain fatty acids, which may be implicated in insulin resistance, and some amino acids are fermented to produce metabolites which can have pro-inflammatory effects.

As well as eating fibre, it's also important to prioritise including as many different plant-based products as possible on your plate. Aim for at least thirty every week! This is necessary because different bacterial species require different nutrients to flourish, so we need to provide them with a range of different fuels.

It can also be helpful to consume polyphenol-rich foods. Polyphenols are naturally occurring chemicals which are found in fruits, vegetables and some drinks. In plants, they often have a role in protecting the plant against UV light or harmful invaders. Research has shown that a diet which is high in polyphenols reduces the risk of diabetes, high blood pressure, heart disease, obesity, neurodegenerative disorders and some cancers. Polyphenols are also good for our gut bacteria. They are poorly absorbed by our gastrointestinal tract, which means that they spend a lot of time present within our large bowel. They can alter the composition of the gut microbiome, promoting the growth of beneficial species and reducing the numbers of harmful species. They may also enhance the quality of the intestinal barrier and modulate inflammation. Some of the best polyphenol-rich foods and drinks include dark berries, red onion, spinach, raw cacao powder, dark chocolate, coffee and red wine.

What about Dairy?

Dairy products are a group of foods and drinks that are made from milk, which has usually come from a cow, sheep or goat. They include cheese, yoghurt and kefir. Some research has shown that increased dairy intake is associated with an increase in microbiome diversity; however, the changes seen might depend on which foods are being consumed. For example, one study found that yoghurt increases diversity, while milk seemed not to. When the bacterial changes occur, this has been reported to be associated with changes in some of the risk factors for heart disease – for example, triglycerides ('bad' fats) in the blood can decrease and high-density lipoprotein (HDL, the 'good' fat) can increase, both of which may confer protection against heart disease.

But the research findings are not consistent. Some studies have found that dairy has no effect, whilst others have reported that it may have an adverse impact on gut bacterial richness or composition. One of the big problems is that many of the studies have varied considerably in how they have been performed. For example, how many people have been part of the study, the type of foods that have been examined and their quantity, the starting state of participants' microbiomes and dairy intake, and whether the study has been a 'snapshot' picture of a population or a long-term project.

The picture isn't completely clear, and more research is needed. A Mediterranean-style diet is often regarded as being the most healthy. This typically includes a small amount of dairy products. If you do choose to eat dairy, try to choose products which are minimally processed and organic, and which are consumed alongside an abundance of plant-based, fibre-fuelled foods.

Meat Substitutes

Over the last decade, meat consumption in the UK has decreased by nearly 20%. This has gone hand in hand with an increase in the amount of meat substitutes eaten. Meat substitutes are typically made from protein extracted from plants such as soy or peas. They also include products made from mycoprotein (derived from fungi) or mushrooms. Many, but not all, meat alternatives have additional chemical ingredients added to make them look, taste and feel more like meat. They include non-meat burgers, sausages, meatballs and mince.

The impact of meat substitutes on the gut microbiome is another area which is currently understudied. At the time of writing, there was only one published study which had addressed this issue. A research group had looked at twenty participants and compared them to a control group of nineteen people. Participants were requested to replace a minimum of four animal-protein-based meals with a plant-based meal each week for four weeks. The meat substitute was generally based on pea protein. Participants and control subjects had their poo analysed before and after the dietary intervention.

The results weren't very dramatic. Overall, there wasn't a significant change in gut diversity for the participants after the intervention. However, there was a reduction in a specific bacterium and there was an increase in the 'good' butyrate-production pathways. The group concluded that *we were able to confirm that the PBMA [plant-based meat alternatives] products provided to participants in the intervention group elicited changes in their gut microbiota that are consistent with eubiosis, i.e. 'a healthy gut microbiome', meaning that the occasional replacement of animal meats with PBMA products seen in flexitarian dietary patterns may promote positive changes to the gut microbiome of consumers.*

In the future, more work needs to be done to dive deeper into the effects that meat substitutes have on the microbiome, including products with different protein bases and with different added ingredients.

Protein

Protein is a vital part of a healthy diet. It has many functions within our body, including growth and repair. Proteins are made from amino acids, some of which we can synthesise, others we need to get through our diet. Sources of protein include meat, fish, dairy, beans, nuts, seeds, chickpeas and green vegetables. Proteins differ in their structure and function depending on their amino acid composition. Many protein-containing foods will also contain other nutrients – for example, legumes such as beans and lentils are rich in fibre, red meat contains iron and saturated fat, and dairy products are often high in calcium.

There are several factors that come into play when we consider the effects that protein has on the microbiome. For example, the amount consumed, its source (red meat, white meat, fish or plant-derived), the extent to which it has been processed and the other nutrients it is being eaten alongside. Gut bacteria use undigested amino acids from proteins to assemble their own microbial components and as an energy source through fermentation. Some of the metabolic products resulting from fermentation can have beneficial effects for the human host while others are harmful.

There is some evidence that suggests that long-term high-protein diets can be harmful to our health, and may increase the risk of inflammatory bowel disease, type 2 diabetes, obesity and cardiovascular disease. When proteins are fermented in the large bowel, the chemicals produced include indoles, phenols, polyamines, hydrogen sulphide, amines and carnitine–some of which may be pro-inflammatory or may affect metabolism. For example, L-carnitine is converted by our gut bacteria into a chemical which ultimately increases the risk of arteries 'furring up' and heart disease. However, other studies have found that proteins, especially soy proteins, which contain all essential amino acids, support the growth of beneficial bacteria.

Proteins from different sources contain different amino acids, fatty acids and pollutants, all of which can affect our gut bacteria. Casein, a milk protein, and other dairy products, contain high amounts of branched-chain fatty acids, and have been shown to reduce the risk of obesity in rodents. Plant-based proteins have a high fibre content and have also been shown to protect against the development of obesity. Generally, consuming proteins from meat has been shown to increase the risk of obesity as opposed to eating protein from seafood or vegetables. Further research is needed to ascertain to what extent the microbiome plays a role in this.

Although the picture isn't completely clear, we do know that protein is a vital component of our diet, but that it should be consumed in moderation and not at the expense of complex carbohydrates/fibre. It may be sensible to try and focus on plant-derived proteins as part of a mixed and varied diet.

Who Are the Bad Guys in Our Diets?

We have seen that fibre and plant diversity are the cornerstones of a healthy gut microbiome, so who are the bad guys? What should we be avoiding or limiting in order to help our bacteria to thrive?

· Ultra-Processed Foods, Sugar and Fat

Our eating patterns have changed dramatically over the last century. In the Western world, well over half of our daily calorie intake comes from ultra-processed foods, which comprise calories and chemicals, but which have very little, if any, nutrient value. Food processing is an umbrella term, which encompasses any change made to raw food. The

University of Sao Paola, Brazil, devised the NOVA food classification system, which groups foods according to the extent to which they have been processed:

Group 1 – Unprocessed or minimally processed foods. These foods that have come directly from plants or animals, or which have undergone processes such as cleaning, removing inedible parts, drying, freezing or pasteurising. Nothing is added. For example: fruit, vegetables, meat, legumes, milk.

Group 2 – Processed culinary ingredients. These are foods which have been extracted from natural foods or nature using techniques such as pressing, grinding, crushing and refining. These foods are usually used to season and cook food. For example: olive oil, seed oils, salt, butter, coconut fat.

Group 3 – Processed foods. These are foods which have been made by adding substances such as salt, butter, oil (Group 2) to natural or minimally processed foods (Group 1), usually to preserve them or to make them tastier. Most of these have just two or three ingredients. For example: vegetables preserved in vinegar, tomato purée with added salt.

Group 4 – Ultra-processed foods. These are substances which may contain substances extracted from foods (such as oils, fats or sugar), or derived from food constituents (for example, hydrogenated fats) or which are synthesised in laboratories from flavour enhancers, colouring agents and other artificial ingredients. Ultra-processed foods include: ready meals, burgers, pizza, breakfast cereals, ice cream.

A diet which is high in ultra-processed foods is associated with obesity and an increased risk of developing diseases such as heart disease, type 2 diabetes, depression and certain cancers. Importantly, an ultra-processed diet is bad for our gut bugs. In 2021, the PREDICT study identified fifteen 'good' bacteria and fifteen 'bad' bacteria (we now know there are fifty 'good' and fifty 'bad' bacteria), which affect parameters such as inflammation, weight and blood sugar control. Research has shown that there is a strong association between ultra-processed food and having more of the 'bad' bugs.

As you might expect, ultra-processed foods often contain high levels of sugar and fat, and with our Western diets we get a 'double whammy' effect – our way of eating is generally low in fibre, which is a bad thing, but fat and sugar also have their own independent, harmful effects. High-fat diets are associated with raised levels of secondary bile acids in our intestines, which can promote the growth of certain bacteria that cause inflammation. They can also increase the levels of bacteria that are very efficient at harvesting energy from our food, which is associated with obesity. Similarly, high-sugar diets also cause dysbiosis, and result in increased numbers of bacteria that have pro-inflammatory effects, along with a reduced capacity for regulating epithelial integrity and mucosal immunity. High levels of sugar can also enhance the abundance of bacterial species which are able to break down the intestinal mucus barrier.

· Sweeteners and Emulsifiers
Sweeteners may also cause problems for our gut, as may emulsifiers. Sweeteners are designed to do what they say on

the tin – to make food or drinks taste sweeter, sometimes up to 20,000 fold. Most sweeteners are not absorbed into our bodies, so the original thought was that would enhance the flavour of food, but they would pass through our intestinal tracts as inert substances. However, we now know that this is not true.

Sweeteners may be natural, such as steviol, or synthetic, such as saccharin. Some are nutritional, which means they have calorific value. Some sweeteners, but not all, have been associated with dysbiosis. Human studies have found that there is a correlation between the amount of sweetener consumed and certain bacterial species which have pro-inflammatory effects. However, not all studies have reported the same findings, so this is another area that needs more research. Sweeteners may also be associated with impaired glucose tolerance, i.e. how efficiently our bodies can dispose of a glucose load, and with weight gain.

Emulsifiers are agents which help to mix two substances that wouldn't usually combine–for example, oil and water. They are often added to food to maintain their texture and prolong their shelf life. Studies in rodent models, and laboratory-based studies, have found that most emulsifiers can reduce the numbers of gut bacteria and reduce their diversity, and some emulsifiers increase the activity of genes involved in inflammation.

How Rapidly Do We See Changes in the Composition of the Microbiome?

If we change our diet, we can see changes in the composition of the microbiome pretty rapidly. Studies haves shown that within a day of different foods reaching the colon, there is a significant change in the composition of the microbiome. However, these changes are only maintained whilst we stick to a new eating pattern. If we revert back to old ways of eating, the microbial composition will revert to its prior state within one to two days.

It's also important to be aware that changes aren't necessarily guaranteed, and are dependent on an individual, including their genetic make-up, environmental factors and the starting state of their microbiome. For example, one study found that a dietary intervention with barley kernel fibre changed the composition of the gut microbiome in a way that led to improved glucose metabolism. However, not everyone responded, and this was found to be due to the initial abundance of a specific species of bacteria, *Prevotella.*

So, What Should I Be Eating?

For optimal gut microbiome health, I recommend…

- Eat at least thirty different plant-based products a week, including fruit, vegetables, nuts, legumes, wholegrains, herbs and spices.
- Eat the rainbow – try and choose as many different coloured products as possible.
- Try to include some polyphenol-rich foods or drinks in your diet every day. Think of dark berries, dark chocolate, coffee, raw cacao or spinach.
- Avoid ultra-processed foods whenever possible, including foods or drinks that contain sweeteners and/ or emulsifiers.
- Enjoy some fermented products daily – you'll hear more about this in the section about probiotics.

- Limit your alcohol intake, although some people may choose to have an occasional glass of red wine! We'll explore this in the next chapter.
- Include protein on your plate but eat it alongside fibre-containing foods and don't eat excessive amounts.
- If you do eat dairy, aim for minimally processed products.

Alcohol

As you might expect, excessive alcohol intake is bad news for our gut bacteria. Studies have shown that alcohol consumption causes bacterial overgrowth in the small bowel, and dysbiosis in the large bowel. We see a change in the composition of the bacteria present, with an increase in potentially harmful species, which produce endotoxins, and a reduction in the 'good' species, which synthesise health-promoting SCFAs.

Alcohol can also increase the permeability of our intestinal barrier, which allows dangerous bacterial products and other substances to enter our circulation and trigger inflammation. For example, chronic alcohol use facilitates an ingress of inflammatory chemical messengers to the liver, which may lead to the progression of a fatty liver (steatosis) to an inflamed and fatty liver (steatohepatitis) and ultimately cirrhosis. Some patients with established cirrhosis can develop 'hepatic encephalopathy' – this describes changes in the brain that cause symptoms such as confusion, forgetfulness, mood and personality changes, and changes in sleeping patterns. It is attributed to systemic inflammation, high levels of a chemical called ammonia in the bloodstream, toxins in the bloodstream and the activation of a type of immune cell in the brain (microglia), all of which are enhanced by dysbiosis and altered function of the microbiome. Alcohol can also impair the immune system in the gut, making us more susceptible to infections.

As well as its directly harmful effects, alcohol may cause problems for our gut through indirect mechanisms. For example, when we've had a tipple, we are more likely to choose unhealthy foods which won't nourish our intestinal ecosystem. Alcohol is also known to disrupt our internal biological clock and sleeping patterns, and this has been shown to exacerbate alcohol-related gut leakiness.

It's not all doom and gloom though! Red wine contains polyphenols, and research has found that drinking red wine promotes the growth of beneficial bacteria and can inhibit the growth of potentially harmful species. Drinking red wine must be done in moderation, though, and many people choose to avoid alcohol altogether.

Interestingly, there is some evidence that both prebiotics (the foods that help our healthy bacteria to thrive) and probiotics (the actual live bacteria themselves) can help to reduce alcohol-induced dysbiosis and alcohol-induced intestinal permeability. So, if you do drink an occasional glass of Merlot, make sure it's accompanied by a meal rich in fibre and fermented foods.

Alcohol and the Gut-Brain Axis

We have seen that our gut and brain communicate with each other. This interaction is affected by alcohol. There is some evidence that alcohol-induced intestinal permeability and certain bacterial products may influence our psychological and cognitive functioning. To illustrate this, one study reported that alcohol-dependent patients with higher measures of gut 'leakiness' also had higher measures of depression, anxiety and alcohol cravings, and scored worse on measures of selective attention. It is possible that these findings are related to the inflammation triggered by changes in the gut. Alcohol-induced dysbiosis may also impact brain activity through changing the activity of the nerves which travel from the gut to the central nervous system.

Lifestyle Factors

There are many other lifestyle factors which can influence the microbiome. These include smoking, exercise, sleep, social connections, stress and time-restricted eating (TRE).

Smoking Cigarettes

Unsurprisingly, our gut bacteria do not like cigarettes, with smokers having reduced bacterial diversity. Similar findings are also reported for people who smoke e-cigarettes. The exact way in which smoking can reduce diversity is not certain, but cigarette smoke contains many toxic substances which enter the bloodstream after the smoke has been inhaled into the lungs. These toxins may have actions in the gut by eliciting antibiotic-like effects, changing the acidity level within the bowel or by altering the production of SCFAs. Research in mice has shown that rodents exposed to cigarette smoke exhibit changes in the composition of their gut microbiome in a way that promotes the development of bowel cancer.

What about Cannabis?

Several countries around the world are legalising cannabis, so it is vital that rigorous research is carried out to further explore its safety. At the moment, the picture isn't clear regarding the impact that cannabis has on the gut microbiome, and its effects may depend on its dose, the method of delivery, frequency of use and the starting state of the microbiome.

Cannabis is a plant-derived drug that can be smoked, eaten or vaped. It contains a compound called THC (delta9 tetrahydrocannabinol), which has an effect on the user's mental state, along with cannabidiol (CBD), which is not psychoactive. Cannabis acts on the 'endocannabinoid system' (ECS), which plays a part in regulating many important processes within our bodies, such as temperature control, eating, our mood and emotional state, inflammation and immunity, sleep, learning and memory. In the gut, the ECS affects the way the bowel contracts, inflammation and helps to maintain the intestinal barrier.

When cannabis is used, studies in mice have shown that there is a reduction in the number of bacteria that are associated with obesity, and there is enhanced abundance of species that can modify fat metabolism to enhance weight loss. There may be increased levels of the SCFAs that can promote immune function. However, other research groups have reported that cannabis changes the composition of the microbiome in a way that promotes inflammation and potentially impairs the integrity of the intestinal barrier. Furthermore, research in humans has also suggested that cannabis users have a specific pattern of bacteria present, which results in less antioxidant protection along with reduced production of beneficial SCFAs, which can lead to cognitive defects.

Although it is seen that cannabis does affect the gut microbiome, further studies are needed to better characterise this, and what it means for an individual.

Exercise

Movement and physical activity have a myriad of benefits for our health and well-being, and they're good for our gut bugs as well!

There have been relatively few studies looking at the impact of exercise on the microbiome compared to diet, and it's important to be aware that these have all differed in terms of their research protocols. For example, the gender of participants, their ages, background activity levels (athletes vs those who are sedentary) and the type of exercise carried out. However, despite the variability in the studies, the general consensus is that cardiovascular exercise increases the diversity of our gut microbiome and its functional capacity, but the exact effect seen may depend on an individual's starting body mass index (BMI), and the type, intensity and duration of the activity undertaken.

Exercise promotes microbial diversity, and can improve the *Bacteroidetes-Firmicutes* ratio, which potentially helps with weight loss. Physical activity also stimulates the growth of bacteria that modulate immunity within the gut and that improve integrity of the intestinal barrier. Furthermore, exercise stimulates bacteria that produce beneficial SCFAs that protect against gastrointestinal disorders and bowel cancer.

For example, it has been shown that a group of international-level rugby players had a significantly greater gut microbiome diversity compared to a control group. This was reflected by relative increases in the activity of pathways involved in amino acid synthesis and carbohydrate metabolism, and faecal levels of SCFAs associated with fitness and overall health. In a study of 'non athletes', cardiorespiratory fitness was shown to correlate with increased microbial diversity, and the microbial profiles of fit individuals favoured the production of butyrate, which is associated with overall health.

Whilst moderate activity levels have a positive effect on microbial composition, high-intensity activity may increase the permeability of the intestinal barrier, which includes a reduction in the thickness of the gut mucus. Similarly, the abundance of butyrate-producing bacteria is decreased in ultramarathon runners, which is accompanied by decreased butyrate levels in the intestine and an impact on host immunity. Whilst activities that cause our heart rates to rise and our breathing rates to increase have a beneficial effect on the gut microbiome, not all exercise has the same effect. For example, it has been reported that resistance (strength) training doesn't have a noticeable impact.

The effect that exercise has can depend on an individual's starting weight. For example, one study found that exercise could increase faecal concentrations of SCFAs in lean, but not obese, participants. A fitness intervention was shown to change the composition of the gut microbiome and rate of SCFA production, along with body composition in lean individuals, whilst these changes were not seen in the obese participants, although their fitness did improve.

It's also important to remember that exercise and physical activity have many other benefits. For example, they can reduce stress levels and improve sleep, and these changes also have a positive impact on our intestinal ecosystem.

Sleep

Sleep is another lifestyle factor which can affect our gut microbiome. Both sleep fragmentation and short sleep duration are associated with gut dysbiosis. It is known that sleep disturbance is associated with metabolic diseases such as diabetes, and one possible mechanism for this is related to the overgrowth of certain gut bacteria, which is seen with poor sleep. The relationship between sleep and the microbiome is a reciprocal one. With dysbiosis, there can be reduced integrity of the intestinal barrier, which allows harmful metabolites to enter our bodies to trigger inflammation and affect immune function. These metabolites can also stimulate activity in the nerves that talk to our brains and all of these factors can aggravate insomnia.

Whilst poor sleep can lead to poor gut health, research has shown that total microbiome diversity is positively correlated with increased sleep efficiency and total sleep time.

Similar to exercise, sleep has several indirect ways in which it impacts the microbiome – for example, when we are well rested, we are more likely to engage in physical activity and to make healthier food choices.

Social Connections

In 2014, an article published in Global News stated that:

> *When you kiss your date, his or her germs make their way into your mouth's ecosystem. And if it's a match, you'll want to keep smooching... it shows you that kissing is the best way to find a mate for the long term. It might sound really gross but if the bacteria from the other person harmonizes with your bacteria, your immune system is all good. You feel a sense of calm and happiness, maybe even addiction, but if the bacteria don't align with your microbes, you actually feel disgust and revolt. Your immune system is rejecting that person as a possible mate.*

The study that the article was referring to had indeed found that eighty million bacteria could be transferred during a ten-second intimate kiss, but the notion that 'bacterial harmonisation' could create positive emotions or that our immune system selects a future partner had been fabricated. However, there is evidence that our social connections and their quality are related to the gut microbiome.

Individuals who live with a spouse or partner have more similar microbiota composition compared to a random stranger, as we may well expect, and they also have greater microbiome diversity than those people who live alone. But the quality of the relationship is also important. Couples who describe their relationship as being 'very close' have greater diversity than those who feel they are 'somewhat close'. These findings are independent of diet but may be related to the sharing of microorganisms through physical contact, and also due to a greater engagement in health-promoting behaviours, such as exercise or reduced stress levels. Going hand in hand with this, we find that loneliness may be associated with dysbiosis. For example, one study looked at 184 adults between the ages of twenty-eight and ninety-seven years of age. The study participants reported their levels of loneliness, wisdom, compassion, social support and social engagement, and it was found that those who were the least lonely had greater gut bacterial richness and diversity.

Stress

Dr Collette Stadler, GP
Dr Lukas Stadler, Biochemical Research Scientist
Dr Emma Short

It is well established that our mental health has an impact on our gut health. Most of us have experienced this first hand–for example, when we are anxiously anticipating an exam or interview, we may feel 'butterflies' in our stomach or suffer from loose stools. Similarly, living through prolonged periods of stress can affect our bowel movements and can cause other gastrointestinal issues, such as heartburn. When we encounter a stressful event, this activates a variety of neural and hormonal pathways which allow us to deal with the stressor. Throughout evolution, the stressor may well have been an attack by a predator: our physiological responses help us to fight the beast or flee to a place of safety. Our stress responses also impact our gut bacteria. When we are stressed, our sympathetic nervous system sends signals to our gut, and stress hormones can reach our intestines through our blood vessels. Furthermore, stress responses may also include an inflammatory component. As a result of these factors, stress leads to enhanced intestinal permeability, increased growth of harmful bacteria and reduced abundance of beneficial species. These detrimental changes have been observed with both acute (sudden) and chronic (long-term) stressful events.

Interestingly, the composition of our gut microbiome plays a role in how we respond to stressors. Research has shown that certain bacterial profiles are related to specific patterns of brain activation when individuals are exposed to emotional stimuli. Other studies have reported that probiotic supplementation can reduce stress and cortisol levels, and research in individuals suffering from chronic fatigue syndrome has shown that probiotics can lead to improvements in some anxiety measures. Similar results, in terms of anxiety reduction, were found when prebiotics were given to patients with irritable bowel syndrome. Some research groups have even reported that specific bacterial species, namely *Lactobacillus plantarum*, are able to alleviate feelings of anxiety.

It is also important to highlight that when we are stressed, this also impacts what we eat, our sleeping patterns and our social interactions, and all of these also have a role to play in the composition of our gut microbiome.

Time-Restricted Eating

Dr Milli Raizada, GP and Lifestyle Medicine Physician,
Dr Emma Short

Time-restricted eating (TRE), also known as Intermittent Fasting (IF), has become a very popular eating pattern over recent years, largely due to its recognised ability to improve a vast range of health and well-being-related parameters. TRE is used as a tool in weight management and has also been shown to improve metabolism, reduce inflammation, enhance brain function, potentially reduce the risk of some cancers, improve blood sugar control, improve blood pressure and slow the effects of ageing.

The term 'TRE' means different things to different people, but, essentially, its focus is not *what* is eaten, but rather *when* food is consumed. Strictly speaking, all food and calories should be taken on board within a specific time frame. For example, someone may choose to eat between midday and 8pm, so that all food is consumed within an eight-hour window. During the sixteen-hour fast, only water, black tea, black coffee and green tea are allowed.

TRE has also been demonstrated, in both animal and human studies, to have a positive impact on our gut microbiome. Fasting can increase microbial diversity and encourages microbiome remodelling, so that the abundance of beneficial species increases. When these changes occur, this is associated with increased activity of a gene that is involved in reducing fat accumulation and reducing the levels of fat which surround our internal organs (visceral fat). The microbiota changes are also associated with an increase in the levels of HDL (high-density lipoprotein), also known as 'good fat', in the bloodstream. These effects may partly explain how TRE has a positive impact on metabolic health. There is also some evidence that intermittent fasting changes the gut microbiome in such a way that there is a reduction in inflammation throughout the body and enhanced functioning of the intestinal barrier.

How Long Is the Ideal Fasting Period?

This is an interesting question and it's best to say we don't yet know the answer to this. Only a small amount of research into TRE and the gut microbiome has been done in human studies. Some research has shown that fasts of twelve to fourteen hours are beneficial, other research was based on sixteen-hour fasts. The water is also muddied by the fact that some studies didn't find any positive effects with TRE on gut bacteria. At the present time, it's fairest to say that there is promising evidence that TRE helps to nurture our intestinal ecosystem, but that more research is needed to dive deeper into the optimum feeding regime and its mechanistic effects.

Prebiotics and Probiotics

Prebiotics and probiotics frequently feature in the media and are often touted as 'miracle cures' for a variety of diseases and ailments. But what exactly are they?

Prebiotics are the fuels that can be used by beneficial microbes. They are the fibre and resistant starches that have been described in the section about nutrition. Prebiotics are food components that we can't digest, but which nourish our healthy gut bacteria. Some of the foods with the best reputation as prebiotics include asparagus, Jerusalem artichoke, garlic, onions and leek.

Probiotics are the actual live organisms themselves. The formal definition of probiotics according to the World Health Organisation is:

> *Live microorganisms which when administered in adequate amounts confer a health benefit on the host.*

Probiotics include certain foods and drinks. For example, yoghurt, sauerkraut, kimchi, kombucha and kefir, and they are also available as supplements. They usually include members of the *Lactobacillus* or *Bifidobacterium* families. It's very important to be aware that probiotics are not regulated as a drug or medicine, and they are widely available in supermarkets, health food shops and through the internet. If we take probiotics, live bacteria may not always reach our intestines, as they can be destroyed by stomach acid and digestive enzymes. If the bacteria do survive their hazardous journey, they may not actually colonise our guts or take up permanent residence. Rather, they can positively influence our microbiome by stimulating the growth of our 'good bacteria' by supplying nutrients, by modulating the pH of our gut and through indirect effects on our intestinal epithelial cells or immune cells. They can also compete with harmful bacterial species for nutrients and some produce antibiotic-like molecules.

Several studies have explored whether probiotics could be used to prevent or treat a range of different diseases. There is some evidence that probiotics do have beneficial effects. For example, it has been reported that probiotics can reduce the duration of infectious diarrhoea, they may reduce the frequency of colds, they can have a positive impact on mood disorders and they may improve eczema. In addition to this, some probiotics have been found to enhance the functioning of the immune system, to reduce intestinal permeability, to reduce inflammation or to improve the antioxidant potential of the gut microbiome.

However, research findings are not always consistent. Some of the reasons for this are that different studies use different species and strains of probiotic bacteria, different doses, different dosing regimens and the studies have been carried out in different patient populations.

Probiotics may not be suitable for everyone, and the general feeling is that they should be avoided by the elderly and anyone who is immunocompromised in any way.

How to Choose a Probiotic

If you go into a store or shop online, the vast range of probiotics available to purchase can seem rather overwhelming. The first thing to ask yourself is *why* you want to take a supplement. Do you have a specific condition that you are hoping to improve, or are you aiming to nurture your gut microbiota in general? If you have a certain disease or illness, it is really worth taking your time to look into what research has been done with the specific supplements that you are looking at for that particular health issue. You don't want to waste your money on a supplement that may do nothing. It's worth knowing that a 'species' of bacteria is a bit like its family name and that a 'strain' is a subtype of a species, so 'The Jones Family' would be the species and the individual family members, Fred Jones, Mary Jones and Lucy Jones, are the strains. If supplements advertise the species they contain, for example *Lactobacillus*, you also need to know which specific strains are present,–for example, *Lactobacillus acidophilus*–and in what quantity.

To help you choose a product that could help you, nutritionist Adrienne Benjamin has outlined what to look out for in a probiotic supplement:

- Clearly defined bacterial strain numbers – every reputable strain will be given a unique number.
- Guaranteed bacteria count to the expiry date of the product.
- Scientific research supporting the individual product and the bacterial strains it contains.
- Evidence that the bacteria can survive both stomach and bile acids and reach the intestines where they can be utilised.
- The bacteria should be able to survive at room temperature.
- The bacterial strains present should be those which are found naturally in the human gastrointestinal tract.
- Evidence of safety, both via research and through positive independent customer reviews.
- The product should be manufactured to current good manufacturing practice (cGMP) guidelines.

Quick-Fire Questions!

As I was writing this book, I was asked many gut-related questions by my family, friends, colleagues and members of the public. I've included some of the most common questions below. Several have been answered by some of the UK's leading experts on the gut microbiome. Please do get in touch if you'd like to ask me anything else!

What are some of the common bacteria found in the human gut and what do they do?

Dr Daniel John, Microbiology Research Scientist

The human gut is home to trillions of bacteria and every person has a completely unique population. Some of the most common bacteria found in Western populations include:

- **Akkermansia muciniphila**: This bacterium is thought to play a role in strengthening the gut lining, preventing excessive gut permeability and protecting against conditions such as diabetes, inflammation and obesity. Its potential role in bowel tumours is being investigated.

- **Bacteroides species**: *Bacteroides* play an important role in breaking down different food components, such as complex carbohydrates. They also produce vitamins such as Vitamin B12 and Vitamin K, and they help to regulate the immune system. However, *Bacteroides* can also cause inflammation if they overgrow or enter the bloodstream.

- **Bifidobacteria species**: *Bifidobacteria* are among the most abundant bacteria in heathy infant guts but are less frequent in adults. They help to digest fibre and complex carbohydrates, they produce beneficial metabolites such as vitamins and SCFAs, they help to boost our immune responses and they play a role in protecting us against potentially harmful bacteria.

- **Clostridium species**: *Clostridium* can support overall gut health through the production of beneficial metabolites such as butyrate. They can also modulate immune responses, inflammation, metabolism and the gut-brain axis. However, some species of *Clostridium* are potentially harmful, such as *Clostridium difficile* (*C. diff*), which is the bacteria that causes 'antibiotic associated diarrhoea'.

- **Enterococcus species**: Some *enterococci* species, such as *Enterococcus faecium*, may have beneficial effects in our guts, including reducing the risk of harmful bacteria-causing infections, modulating our immune system and producing vitamins such as Vitamin B12 and folate. However, other members of the family can cause urinary infections.

- **Eschericia Coli (*E. Coli*)**: *E. coli* is one of the best known bacteria and some strains can cause food poisoning.

However, most strains of *E. coli* are harmless and some are beneficial, producing vitamins such as B and K Vitamins, helping with iron absorption and boosting our immune response.

- **Faecalibacterium prausnitzii** is considered a biomarker of a healthy gastrointestinal tract and it plays a key role in overall gut health. It has anti-inflammatory properties, enhances the function of the intestinal barrier, is involved in the regulation of glucose metabolism and boosts our immune responses.

- **Klebsiella species** have been linked to various gastrointestinal diseases, including Crohn's, ulcerative colitis and bowel cancer. Some of their effects are mediated through triggering inflammation within the gut.

- **Lactobacillus species** have many health-promoting roles in the gut. They belong to the *Firmicutes* family. They produce lactic acid, which lowers the pH within the bowel to inhibit the growth of harmful bacteria, they enhance immune responses and they are associated with a reduced risk of inflammatory bowel disease and type 2 diabetes.

All of these bacteria fall into five main groups or phyla: *Bacteroidetes* (*Bacteroidota*), *Firmicutes* (*Bacillota*), *Actinobacteria* (*Actinomycetota*), *Proteobacteria* (*Pseudomonadota*) and *Verrucomicrobia*. Of these, *Bacteroidetes* and *Firmicutes* are usually the most common in the human gut. The *Firmicutes/Bacteroidetes* (F/B) ratio is widely accepted to have an important influence in maintaining a heathy gut with an increase in F/B being associated with weight gain and obesity. Studies have suggested that exercise, increasing fibre intake and eating less fat and sugar can help to improve the F/B ratio.

What impact do antibiotics have on the microbiome? Should we take a probiotic supplement if we receive a course of antibiotics?

Dr Daniel John, Microbiology Research Scientist

Antibiotics have revolutionised the treatment of bacterial infections due to their ability to inhibit the growth of bacteria or to destroy bacteria. Without a doubt, their use has saved countless lives. However, they can have a negative impact on the gut microbiome. Broad-spectrum antibiotics, which are active against a wide range of species, can reduce the overall number and diversity of gut bacteria, which includes reducing protective species such as *Bifidobacterium* and *Lactobacillus*. This effectively leaves a 'gap' that can potentially be filled by harmful microorganisms, including bacteria, fungi or viruses. Studies have shown that after short-term antibiotic use, it can take at least one to two months for most bacterial groups to recover to pre-antibiotic levels. Antibiotic-related dysbiosis can affect an individual in several ways, including impacting immune regulation, mental health and metabolism, which is partly explained through a reduction in SCFAs.

One key question is how do we minimise the damage that antibiotics cause to the gut microbiome? One potential solution would be to consume a probiotic alongside or just after taking antibiotic therapy. Some studies have shown that probiotics can reduce the negative impact that antibiotics have and can help to preserve bacterial diversity. They may help to restore populations of friendly bacteria such as *Lactobacillus, Bifidobacterium* and *Faecalibacterium prausnitzii*, which reduces inflammation and promotes a healthy intestinal barrier. However, not all research supports this approach, with some evidence suggesting that probiotics can actually delay the recovery of the microbiome, in such a way that it doesn't completely return to its pre-antibiotic state.

Dietary modulation is another way to help restore the microbiome. Fermented foods such as yogurts, kimchi, sauerkraut and kombucha have been shown to help promote the growth of beneficial bacteria, along with foods high in fibre such as wholegrains, nuts, seeds, lentils, broccoli, peas and bananas.

Antibiotics are vital and life-saving drugs used to treat bacterial infections that unfortunately have unintended negative consequences within our intestines. At the current time, it is clear that more research is needed to explore ways to reduce these side effects and to promote a healthy gut microbiome.

What impact do commonly used medications such as ibuprofen have on the microbiome?

Whilst it's obvious that antibiotics will impact the gut microbiome, as they are designed to target bacteria, you might be surprised to learn that many medications commonly used and prescribed in the UK also have an effect within our gut. One study looked at over a thousand drugs and their impact on forty different strains of gut bacteria. The study reported that 24% of the drugs with human targets could inhibit the growth of at least one bacterial strain in experiments performed in the laboratory. It was noted that this figure is likely to be an underestimate, as only a small number of bacterial species were included in the experiments, and there were very strict experimental criteria.

Some of the drugs that have been shown to affect the gut microbiome include aspirin, celecoxib, ibuprofen, proton-pump inhibitors such as omeprazole, paracetamol, opioids and certain antidepressants. It's generally found that specific medications are associated with distinct microbial populations. However, it's very important to be aware that certain medications are taken for specific diseases, so it can be hard to untangle the extent to which the microbiome changes are disease related or drug related.

It is clear that the medicines we use can shape the composition of our gut microbiome. In turn, our gut bacteria are also known to modulate how effective some drugs are and their side effects. For example, Metformin is a medication used in the management of type 2 diabetes. Research has shown that it has a rapid effect on the composition and function of the gut microbiome, in a way that results in a change in metabolic parameters such as HbA1C and fasting blood glucose levels.

How can we encourage parents and children to eat more vegetables?

Encouraging children to develop healthy eating habits from an early age is vitally important. Currently, almost one in five children are obese when they leave primary school. Sugary drinks account for 30% of four-to ten-year-olds' daily sugar intake and ultra-processed foods make up more than 60% of the calories consumed by British children. These eating habits can make children feel sluggish and lethargic, and they create a ticking time bomb for the development of chronic diseases in later life.

Most parents will understand that encouraging children to eat more vegetables (along with fruits, nuts, legumes, etc.) is not always easy. We want to try and create healthy habits which are simple, enjoyable and inexpensive. Some of my strategies are:

• **Establish what a child already enjoys eating and make healthy tweaks.** We are aiming to increase intake of plant-based products, but we want to do this in a way that creates little resistance from our little ones! If you find the foods that children enjoy, you can make small changes or additions to them to make them healthier. The same is true for adults. In the table below, I have listed some of the meals that a group of my friends said that their families eat on a typical day and have suggested tweaks that would benefit our friendly gut bacteria.

Meal/Food	Healthy Tweak
Porridge and jam	Add a sliced banana Sprinkle with seed mix
Cheese and ham roll	Add sliced tomato or lettuce Use wholemeal bread

Cheese and tomato pizza	Add sweetcorn or mushrooms on top Serve with chopped cucumber and carrots
Pasty and chips	Choose a vegetable pasty Eat a piece of fruit afterwards
Sausage and mash	Make the mash with parsnips as well as potatoes Have a side portion of peas and carrots
Chicken breast and green salad	Add tomatoes, pine nuts and a seed mix to the salad
Bagel with soft cheese	Choose a wholemeal bagel, add sliced tomato
Cheese and biscuits	Eat with grapes
Spaghetti bolognaise	Finely dice carrots, mushrooms and peppers and add to the sauce
Chicken nuggets and chips	Include a side serving of beans or peas and broccoli
Baked potato, beans and cheese	Mix in kidney beans and/or black beans with the baked beans
Ice cream	Create an ice cream sundae by adding chopped strawberries and banana

- **Involve children in preparing food.** Children love to help out in the kitchen and it is fantastic if you involve them in all stages of food preparation. When you're in the supermarket, let them choose fruits and vegetables to try, encourage them to find new recipes and help them to chop and dice. Children are more likely to eat a healthy meal if they have been involved in cooking it.

- **Finely chop and 'hide' vegetables or fruits.** Depending on the age of the child, it can be helpful to cut up vegetables into such tiny pieces that they don't realise they're eating them! For example, a range of vegetables can be chopped (or even blended) to make a delicious pasta sauce – onions, garlic, mushrooms, courgette, peppers and tomatoes. Similarly, fruit smoothies can be a great way to increase diversity in our diets, and they can be used to 'hide' bland vegetables such as cauliflower or avocado. (For a recipe book packed with healthy smoothie options, check out *Smoothie Doctors*!)

- **Offer choices.** Children go through different developmental phases, and at different times they may have a need to try and exert their autonomy. By offering them a simple choice, i.e. 'Would you like cauliflower or broccoli, to go with your meal?', you are nurturing their independence, whilst still being in control of their nutrition.

- **Teach your children about their gut microbiome!** In my experience, many children and adults are more prepared to look after their amazing intestinal ecosystem than they are to look after themselves. When making food choices, ask, 'Do you think your gut bugs would enjoy this? Will it help them to grow and thrive so that they can look after you? Is there anything else you could choose that your microbiome would prefer?' I know several children who think of their gut bacteria as their own special pets!

What are poo transplants? Can they be used to cure disease?

I promise this isn't as unpleasant as it sounds! Poo transplants (formally known as faecal microbiota transplants, or FMT) involve taking the poo from a healthy person (the donor) and transplanting it into a recipient. The process aims to introduce beneficial bacteria to an individual to help manage or cure a specific disease. Poo donors are screened to ensure that they are healthy and do not carry any infections, and the poo sample is similarly tested. The poo itself is usually given to the recipient in a liquid form, and it can be transplanted via a thin tube which goes into the stomach or small bowel via the nose, or into the large bowel through the anus. Some hospitals are starting to use capsules of poo, which can simply be swallowed.

In the UK, FMT is currently being used to treat recurrent *Clostridium difficile* infections (antibiotic-associated diarrhoea). As we saw above, antibiotics can kill off many of our healthy gut bacteria, and this allows harmful bugs to grow in their place. When this happens, most people will respond to specific antibiotics that target the harmful bacteria, but some patients continue to suffer from loose stools. This happens because the beneficial bacteria don't return to desirable levels, so the dangerous species continue to thrive. In this situation, FMT is very effective in re-establishing a population of healthy bacteria in the bowel.

At the present time, FMT is only being used in the context of antibiotic-associated diarrhoea, but there is a vast amount of research being done across the globe to explore whether it could have a role in treating a wide range of health conditions, including:

- inflammatory bowel disease
- diabetes
- obesity
- anxiety and depression
- autism
- arthritis

Is gut health related to mental health and vice versa?

Dr Ros Marvin, Consultant Palliative Care Physician

Until recently, the idea that our microbiome could influence how we think and feel would have seemed crazy! But we now know that the bacteria in our gut communicate with our brain and our brain talks back, via the microbiome-gut-brain axis. Communication occurs via nerves, chemical messengers, hormones and immunological factors. This means that our mood can influence our gut microbiome, and our microbiome can influence our mood.

Research looking at the impact of the microbiome on mental health is in the early stages, but there have already been numerous studies published with interesting results. For example, it has been shown that germ-free mice, which have been bred and raised in a sterile environment, have altered brain function compared to those with a normal microbiome. Clinical studies in humans have shown that the microbiome composition of people with major depressive disorder, MDD, the leading cause of disability worldwide, is significantly different to people without MDD, and when faecal material from patients with MDD is transplanted into germ-free mice, the mice display depression-like behaviour. Other research involved giving probiotics to healthy volunteers over a thirty-day period. The volunteers experienced reduced levels of the stress hormone cortisol, along with improved psychological well-being, and these changes were similar to those seen in a control group who had been given the anti-anxiety medication diazepam. In addition to this, it has been shown that increased intestinal permeability is associated with several psychiatric disorders and neurodevelopmental disorders, including depression, anxiety and autism. Furthermore, children with autism who underwent a ten-week treatment with faecal microbiota transplantation (FMT) from healthy donors showed improvement in global functioning, social skills and other symptoms of autism, and their average developmental age increased by 1.4 years.

Whilst the studies above specifically studied the gut microbiome, there is a wealth of research which has explored how diet can affect mental health. Given that we now know how closely linked diet is to the gut microbiota, it is reasonable to assume that much of the association between diet and mental well-being is mediated through the impact of diet on the intestinal ecosystem.

A scientific review of twenty studies showed that a high intake of fruit and vegetables, wholegrains, chicken and fish, along with a low intake of ultra-processed food – *in other words, the type of diet that improves the gut microbiome* – was associated with a lower risk of depression. One of those studies randomised patients with moderate to severe depression into two groups. One group received support in following a Mediterranean-style diet, and the other group received social support only. A third of the patients who changed their diet achieved remission of their depression symptoms – compared to only 8% of those in the social support group. This is a far bigger effect than that shown by studies on the efficacy of antidepressants.

What we know from these studies is that by improving gut health, we can improve our mental well-being. By simply increasing our intake of vegetables, fruit, wholegrains and legumes, increasing the diversity in our diets, avoiding ultra-processed foods, and adding in some fermented foods, we can live happier lives.

Is there any relationship between the gut microbiome and menopause?

This is a great question, and it's currently an area which is relatively unexplored. Some of the information I have given below has come from studies in animals, rather than from human research, and some of the human studies had small numbers of participants, which can make research less reliable.

The menopause is defined as twelve months without a menstrual period. As a female approaches the menopause, which is usually described as the 'perimenopausal period', there are changes in the levels of her sex hormones. In a nutshell, oestrogen and progesterone levels fall. This can be associated with a wide range of symptoms, including hot flushes, night sweats, changes in mood, difficulty sleeping, reduced libido and vaginal dryness. Oestrogen has a protective effect on many systems in the body, which means that after the menopause, the risk of developing certain diseases increases for example–osteoporosis and heart disease.

Sex hormones also impact the gut microbiome. Generally, the microbiomes of male and female children are similar in their composition, but when puberty and adolescence hit, there is a divergence in the bacterial species present. By adulthood, there are distinct difference between the gut microbiomes of males and females, with females having greater bacterial richness and lower abundance of bacteria such as *Prevotella*. Whilst these differences may be partially due to the effects of the sex hormones, there are many environmental factors which also play a role.

There is a bidirectional relationship between sex hormones and the gut microbiome – the female sex hormones appear to enhance bacterial diversity and play a role in maintaining the integrity of the intestinal barrier, and, in turn, certain bacteria possess genes that play a role in oestrogen metabolism and which can promote hormone retention, in what is known as the 'oestrobolome'. Oestrogens are modified by the liver before they enter our intestines, so that they can be excreted in our poo. Some of our gut bacteria are able to alter the oestrogens so that they can be reabsorbed and enter our circulation. The same is true for hormones such as progesterone and androgens. Plant-based oestrogens are also metabolised through similar pathways.

At the time of the perimenopause and menopause, when levels of oestrogen fall, this is reflected in the gut by a reduction in bacterial richness, and a shift towards the bacterial composition which is found in males. Furthermore, it is possible that the changes in hormonal levels cause the gut to become more permeable. If potentially harmful substances enter the circulation, this can trigger inflammation, which is associated with several chronic diseases, including obesity. In addition to a reduction in bacterial diversity, there is also a change in the abundance of certain species, which could impact the functional capacity of the microbiota. Menopause-related changes in the gut microbiota also reduce its oestrobolome activity.

The key question, though, is what does all of this mean for women? Although it is evident that the menopause is associated with changes in the gut microbiome, the impact that this actually has needs to be further evaluated. Some studies have shown that menopause-related changes in the gut microbiome are associated with an increased risk of developing heart disease, due to changes in the lipid profile in the blood and higher blood pressure. Other studies have reported that certain probiotics may be helpful in reducing menopausal symptoms, and some research has shown that hormone replacement therapy (HRT) may reduce dysbiosis. However, further research is needed to really understand how changes in the gut microbiome contribute to menopause-related diseases, along with changes in mood and well-being.

What are enterotypes?

When we're talking about enterotypes, the first thing to mention is that this is a slightly controversial area, and I'll explain why after we've looked at what enterotypes actually are!

Enterotypes are a way of classifying individuals based on the composition of their gut microbiome. Generally, it is thought that there are three dominant enterotypes, and these are characterised by which species are especially abundant. Those with enterotype 1 have numerous *Bacteroides* species, and they are also referred to as those with a 'Western' enterotype, as this pattern is typically found in those who have a high intake of processed foods along with protein and animal fat. Enterotype 2 is enriched for *Prevotella* species and these 'vegetable munchers' often consume large amounts of carbohydrates and wholegrains. Finally, enterotype 3 is characterised by richness in *Ruminococcus.*

Different enterotypes are often found in different geographical regions around the world, and this is largely dependent upon the eating patterns of the specific population that lives there.

One of the reasons why enterotypes are particularly interesting is that the different groups are each associated with an increased risk of developing specific diseases. For example, we find higher rates of liver disease, bowel cancer and inflammatory bowel disease in those with enterotype 1, and those with enterotype 2 have an increased risk of high blood pressure and rheumatoid arthritis. This is useful information – if we understand which diseases someone is at risk of developing, we can explore ways to try and reduce this risk.

So, why are enterotypes controversial? The first point to be aware of is that individuals are often classified based on a single analysis of their poo. Whilst this 'snapshot' gives a picture at a given point in time, we have seen that an individual's microbiome can change rapidly when they change their diet. Some people feel that categorisation shouldn't be determined on a single assessment and that the potential fluidity of the microbiome needs to be acknowledged. In this sense, enterotypes can be useful at the population level, but not at the individual level.

Another reason for controversy is that the exact way in which the enterotypes are defined can vary according to the method used for classification. Several researchers feel that there are only two real enterotypes – one with abundant *Prevotella*, and one enriched for *Bacteroides*, with the *Ruminococcus* group being combined with the latter. In addition to this, other research suggests that we shouldn't be trying to stratify bacterial populations at all, because their composition has a continuous spectrum which shouldn't be forced into discrete categories.

As with many aspects of the gut microbiome, this is an area which needs to be further explored so that we can have a greater understanding of different groups (if they really exist!) and how they could be nurtured to promote health and positive well-being.

What is fermented food?

Fermented foods, such as sauerkraut and kimchi, are often recommended as part of a gut-healthy diet due to the live bacteria they contain. They have been a staple food source in many cultures for thousands of years and were originally developed to help preserve food and to increase its flavour.

Fermentation describes a chemical process during which microorganisms convert carbohydrates or sugars into products such as acids or alcohol. Carbon dioxide gas is typically released during the reaction, which explains why fermented foods and drinks can have a fizzy texture. The reaction is carried out without oxygen (anaerobically).

Does spending time in nature affect our gut microbiome?

Absolutely! We know that the environment we live in plays an important role in shaping the composition of our gut microbiome, with people living in urban settings having less microbial diversity than those who live in rural locations. In 2018, a group of researchers in Finland carried out a study looking at how exposure to soil might impact the gut microbiome. Over a two-week period, a group of healthy adults living in an urban environment were tasked with rubbing their hands with soil and plant-derived material three times a day, followed by washing their hands with water. At the end of the intervention, poo analysis showed that gut microbial diversity had increased. The same research group also showed that the plants present in our gardens are important in modelling our intestinal ecosystem, with yard vegetation, especially shrubs and non-woody flowering plants, shifting the relative abundance of *Bacteroides* and *Firmicutes* species to a more favourable ratio.

Studies in children have also highlighted the beneficial effects of spending time in nature. A ten-week 'play and grow' programme, which comprises interaction with the natural outdoor world, resulted in children feeling more connected to nature and less stressed as well as changes in their gut microbiota. There were modulations in the abundance of the friendly bacteria, *Roseburia*, as well as changes in the level of serotonin in faeces.

It is likely that the beneficial effects that are observed result partly from direct exposure to microorganisms, but also through mechanisms such as reduced stress levels.

Interview with Dr Miguel Toribio-Mateas

Whilst I was researching the gut microbiome, I was extremely fortunate to speak to Dr Miguel Toribio-Mateas, one of the UK's top microbiome experts. Below, I've shared one of the conversations we had.

Dr Toribio-Mateas, could you tell us about yourself and your interest in the gut microbiome?

I'm a clinical neuroscientist and applied microbiologist. My DProf (a doctoral degree just like a PhD but with more fieldwork) was spent looking at the impact that fermented foods have on cognitive (brain) functioning. I have always had an interest in mental well-being, and over the years my work has become increasingly focused on the connection between the brain and the gut. For example, considering the role that the microbiome has in neurodevelopmental conditions such as autism, and in exploring how we can promote gut heath in order to enhance mental health.

My work looks at the gut microbiome in the context of parameters such as stress, anxiety, happiness and resilience.

You have published some fascinating research papers, including one which looked at the role of a microbiome-targeted dietary intervention in children with ADHD. We know that the gut can communicate with the brain through bioactive products of the microbiome, inflammation and immunity, hormones and neural activity. Which of these do you think is the most important?

They are all important, but I'd say that the metabolic products of the microbiome are key, especially butyrate. However, all of these mechanisms can potentially interact with each other. For example, when butyrate levels are high, this is associated with improved functioning of the liver, and the liver is involved in regulating the levels of certain hormones. So, it's not always possible to separate one mechanism from another.

What are five ways in which butyrate and other SCFAs influence our brains?

There are lots of ways! These include…

- *As well as crossing the blood-brain barrier, butyrate helps to maintain its integrity, so is important in controlling which molecules and nutrients can enter.*
- *Butyrate modulates inflammatory responses in the brain.*
- *SCFAs may affect levels of neurotransmitters, which are the chemicals that nerves use to communicate with each other.*
- *SCFAs also modulate the levels of chemicals that regulate the growth, survival and differentiation of nerves.*
- *SCFAs affect which genes are turned on and off in the brain and they are involved in memory consolidation, sleeping and appetite.*

Are there particular bacteria that are associated with being happy?

Lactobacillus and Bifidobacteria are the species which are the most respected as being able to modulate mood. They are also the species which are commonly found in fermented products such as kefir. One of their major functions is to lower the pH in the gut, to make it more acidic. This environment stops the growth of potentially harmful bacteria.

How do harmful bacteria affect our brains?

Certain bacteria contain a chemical called lipopolysaccharide (LPS) in their cell walls. LPS can impair the integrity of the intestinal barrier and can trigger inflammation throughout the body. We find that when LPS levels are high, this is associated with more severe symptoms in neurological diseases–for example, Alzheimer's Disease. Furthermore, by impairing the functioning of the intestinal barrier, it means that potentially harmful foods or toxins that we eat can also gain access to our bloodstream, which will further exacerbate inflammation.

Whilst we're considering intestinal permeability, there have been several media articles which have reported that 'Leaky Gut Syndrome' is a cause of several diseases, especially autoimmune disease. What are your thoughts on this?

All guts are 'leaky' as they need to allow nutrients and water to be reabsorbed. In this sense, 'Leaky Gut Syndrome' can't be a diagnosis, as everyone has a leaky gut to some extent, and 'leakiness' varies over the course of the day and is affected by what we eat and drink, infections, medications and several other factors. However, when there is increased gut permeability, or 'leakiness', this can cause inflammation and is potentially associated with a range of chronic diseases.

Increased intestinal permeability can occur when there is dysbiosis, when there is a reduction in the quality or quantity of intestinal mucus and/or when the cells which line the gut aren't as closely adherent to each other as they should be.

There are several ways to measure the 'leakiness' of the gut. One of the simplest techniques is to give someone a specific substance to eat which isn't usually absorbed by the intestines. If the gut is 'leaky' and the substance gains access to the circulation, it will be excreted via the kidneys, so can be detected in urine.

Do you think that our current lifestyles impact our gut microbiome, in terms of using soap to wash our hands, dishwasher detergent, washing powder and so on?
This is an interesting question! We know that different environments affect the composition of our gut microbiome, so that someone living on a rural farm is likely to have a different microbial composition compared to someone living in the city. Studies have shown that certain chemicals found in cleaning products–for example, Triclosan, which is an antibacterial compound in soaps, detergents and hand sanitisers–can be absorbed through the skin and is linked to dysbiosis.

But we must be pragmatic, and we need to balance staying safe with inappropriate overuse of soap and other products. We might need to use bleach to adequately clean the toilet to reduce the risk of harmful infections, but we shouldn't be washing our hands every five minutes.

Simple Swaps

Fuelling our incredible gut microbiome doesn't need to be complicated, time-consuming or expensive. Making small changes can have a big impact. Here are some simple food swaps you might like to try to help your gut bugs to thrive:

Instead of...	Try...
White rice	Brown rice
White pasta	Wholegrain pasta Lentil pasta
White bread	Wholemeal or seeded bread
Pre-prepared tomato sauce for pasta	Passata with a pinch of basil and oregano (it's even more tasty if you add onions and garlic)
Fruit-flavoured yoghurt	Plain Greek yoghurt
Drinking chocolate powder	Raw cacao powder
Shop-bought ice cream	Frozen mashed bananas or sorbet made from mixed mangoes and coconut milk
Pop/fizzy drinks	Kombucha
Shop-bought chips	Roasted potato wedges or sweet potato wedges

Shop-bought salad dressing	Mix together equal parts of olive oil and balsamic vinegar
Chocolate bar	Square of dark chocolate
Porridge with syrup	Porridge with fruit
Iceberg lettuce	Mixed leaves salad
Peanuts	Mixed nuts
Strawberries	Mixed summer fruits

Kitchen Staples

I find it's handy to have a stock of certain items at home, so that you've got everything you need to make a range of gut-healthy meals and snacks. The following items are what I aim to keep in the kitchen – you don't need to have all of them, just a small selection of what you fancy will be great. I've also included my seed mix as a kitchen staple, as I use it all the time on yoghurt, in smoothies and with salads.

Cupboards

- Brown rice
- Wholemeal pasta
- Lentil pasta
- Quinoa
- Seeded bread
- Wholemeal bread
- Sourdough bread
- Red lentils
- Green lentils
- Tinned tomatoes
- Tinned chickpeas
- Tinned butter beans
- Tinned kidney beans
- Chia seeds
- Pumpkin seeds
- Sunflower seeds
- Linseeds
- Golden linseeds
- Pine nuts
- Pistachios
- Dried goji berries
- Raisins
- Sultanas
- Dates
- Cashew nuts
- Mixed nuts

- Peanut butter
- Cashew nut butter
- Porridge oats
- Sauerkraut
- Kimchi

- Coconut milk
- Tahini
- Soy sauce
- Raw cacao powder

Freezer

- Mixed summer fruits
- Blueberries
- Mango
- Mashed bananas

- Peas
- Sweetcorn
- Spinach

Fridge

- Kefir
- Kombucha
- Greek yoghurt
- Onions
- Red onions
- Garlic
- Mixed salad leaves
- Tomatoes
- Peppers

- Courgettes
- Sweet potatoes
- Carrots
- Broccoli
- Parsnips
- Celery
- Strawberries
- Raspberries

Fruit bowl

- Bananas
- Apples
- Satsumas
- Pears

- Kiwi
- Whatever else is in season!

Seed mix

- 150g chia seeds
- 150g golden linseeds
- 150g linseeds
- 150g sesame seeds
- 150g poppy seeds
- Optional: pumpkin seeds, sunflower seeds

Seed mix diversity score = 5 (I'll explain what this means in the next section!) – even more if you include a greater variety of seeds! Mix the seeds and keep in an airtight jar.

Recipes

I don't know if anyone else is like me, but I love recipe books! I have several shelves stacked with collections of delicious treasures. However, I sometimes feel a bit overwhelmed by how many recipes some of the books contain. I tend to try a handful, then the book gets puts to one side, never to be opened again. To keep this book simple and accessible, I've included a small selection of recipe suggestions, each of which will fuel your friendly gut bacteria and help them to thrive. There are enough recipes here for a different breakfast every day for a fortnight, along with a selection of meals that can be enjoyed for lunch or dinner. I've also included a handful of healthy side dishes and desserts. I haven't included portion sizes as I tend to cook a big batch, then freeze whatever is left over for future meals.

When choosing your meals, aim for diversity. I have given each recipe a diversity score based on how many different gut-healthy ingredients it contains. Try and reach a score of at least thirty every week, although you may want to aim even higher, as some ingredients appear in multiple recipes so may be counted more than once.

If you're not used to eating much fibre, it's best if you introduce the meals gradually, and make sure you drink enough water, otherwise you may experience windy or sluggish consequences!

Breakfast

· Porridge and Overnight Oats

Porridge is an absolute staple for a healthy gut. Porridge oats are a fantastic prebiotic that nourish our beneficial bacteria. One of the things I love about porridge is its versatility – you can add many different fruits, spices or nuts to change its flavour and increase your diversity score. The porridge recipes below can also be used to make overnight oats – to do this, prepare them in the evening and leave in the fridge overnight, mixed with a tablespoon of Greek yoghurt.

A basic porridge is simply oats with milk or water (diversity score: 1), or you could premix oats with chia seeds, flaxseeds, linseeds and pumpkin seeds (diversity score: 5). Below are my favourite additions to fuel your intestinal well-being. To all of the recipes, add your milk of choice.

Festive Warmer – Diversity score: 8
- Oats
- 1 grated apple
- 6 cloves
- 1 teaspoon of ground cinnamon
- 1 teaspoon of ground ginger
- 1 teaspoon of ground nutmeg
- Top with peanut butter and a handful of sultanas.

Hug in a Bowl – Diversity score: 6

- Oats
- 8 Medjool dates (finely chopped)
- 2 teaspoons of peanut butter
- 1 tablespoon of raw cacao powder
- 6 pecan nuts
- Top with dried cranberries.

Banana and Cacao – Diversity score: 4

- Oats
- Finely sliced banana
- 2 teaspoons of raw cacao powder
- 2 teaspoons of chia seeds

Fruit Porridge – Diversity score: 5

Dr Collette Stadler

- Oats
- 1 apple and 1 pear, cut into small chunks
- Half a teaspoon of ground cinnamon
- 2 tablespoons of linseeds
- Top with probiotic yoghurt and a drizzle of honey or agave syrup.

Summer Porridge – Diversity score: 7

- Oats
- Quinoa
- 1 teaspoon of pumpkin seeds
- 1 teaspoon of sesame seeds
- 1 teaspoon of chia seeds
- Mango, chopped
- Blueberries

Fruit and Fibre Porridge – Diversity score: 7
- Oats
- 1 teaspoon of chia seeds
- Quinoa
- 1 teaspoon of pumpkin seeds
- 1 teaspoon of sesame seeds
- 2 teaspoons of raw cacao powder
- 1 teaspoon of peanut butter
- Blueberries

Carrot Cake Overnight Oats – Diversity score: 9
This is one of my absolute favourite breakfasts. Soaking the sultanas makes them plump up, and they do a little 'pop' as you bite them.
- Oats
- 1 teaspoon of chia seeds
- 1 grated carrot
- Mixed spice – you can buy this ready-made, or you can make your own mix with equal quantities of cassia, coriander seed, nutmeg, ground ginger and ground cloves.

Mango Overnight Oats – Diversity score: 3
- Oats
- Mango, chopped
- Greek yoghurt
- Top with pecan nuts.

Blueberry 'Jelly' – Diversity score: 13
- 1 cup of blueberries
- 1 tablespoon of chia seeds
- Top up with oat milk.
- Blitz, leave in the fridge overnight.
- Top with a handful of muesli (see recipe below).

Muesli – Diversity score: 12

Find an airtight glass jar and half-fill it with oats.

Top up the remaining half with:

- Sultanas
- Dried cranberries
- Sunflower seeds
- Linseeds
- Chia seeds
- Sesame seeds
- Cashew nuts
- Almonds
- Hazelnuts
- Walnuts
- Pecans
- Shake the jar to mix!

Toast with Peanut Butter and Jam – Diversity score: 10

If you enjoy eating bread, ideally you'd make it at home so you know exactly what's going into it. The next best option would be to buy it from a local baker, as they're less likely to add the preservatives that are often found in the bread from large commercial suppliers. However, we all need to be pragmatic with our food choices, and if we're rushed for time, and need something quick, toasting store-bought bread may be a necessity.

I'd recommend choosing a wholegrain seeded loaf, as these are high in fibre, and typically contain a mixture of linseeds, sunflower seeds, pumpkin seeds, millet seeds, golden linseeds and poppy seeds. A delicious topping is nut butter and chia berry jam:

- 250g raspberries
- 125g strawberries
- 125g blueberries
- 3 tablespoons of honey or agave syrup or maple syrup
- 3 tablespoons of chia seeds

Add the berries and honey to a pan, and heat gently until the berries break down. Add the chia seeds, stir and simmer for 10 minutes. The jam thickens as it cools and can be kept in an airtight jar in the fridge for up to 5 days.

Greek Yoghurt and Berries – Diversity score: 8
- 2 tablespoons of full-fat Greek yoghurt
- Mixed Summer berries – these can often be bought frozen.

Add to the yogurt, then leave in the fridge overnight to defrost. They typically include strawberries, raspberries, blackberries and blueberries. Top with a handful of hazelnuts, pecan nuts and pomegranate seeds.

Banana Pancakes – Diversity score: 4
- 1 banana
- 1 egg
- 1 teaspoon of cinnamon

Blitz together the banana, egg and cinnamon.

To cook the pancake, heat 2 teaspoons of olive oil in a frying pan. Add the pancake batter, and gently cook through. Once the top has started to firm, complete the cooking by putting the pan under a grill (be very careful to not touch a hot handle with your hands). Serve with blueberries and cashew nuts.

Lunches and Dinners

Swede Soup – Diversity score: 3
- Roast 2 beetroots, 1 golden beetroot and a peeled swede. Once cooked, peel the beetroots, put everything into a blender with a tin of coconut milk. Blitz, heat and enjoy!

Winter Soup – Diversity score: 9
In a large pot, boil…
- 500g red lentils
- 1 butternut squash, peeled and diced
- 1 chopped onion
- At least 4 cloves of crushed garlic
- 4 chopped carrots
- 2 chopped red peppers
- 2 teaspoons of turmeric
- 2 teaspoons of cumin

Once cooked through, blitz together, heat, then top with pistachio nuts.

Medicinal Soup (I always enjoy this when I'm feeling run down!) – Diversity score: 7
Boil together:
- 1 cauliflower, chopped
- 1 packet of spinach
- 3 cups of peas

Leave enough of the water to blitz into a thick soup. Heat up and add:
- 2 teaspoons of sumac
- 2 teaspoons of turmeric

- 2 teaspoons of chilli powder
- 2 teaspoons of ground coriander

Mushroom and Lentil Bolognaise – Diversity score: 9

- 1 chopped onion
- At least 4 cloves of crushed garlic
- 1 chopped red pepper
- 250g closed-cap mushrooms, sliced
- 100g chestnut mushrooms, sliced
- 500g red lentils
- Passata
- 2 teaspoons of basil
- 2 teaspoons of oregano

Gently sauté all of the vegetables. Once they've begun to soften, add the lentils, passata and herbs and simmer until the lentils have cooked. Serve with wholegrain or lentil pasta.

Vegetable Tray Bake – Diversity score: 7

- 4 sticks of celery, chopped into thick slices
- Diced sweet potato
- Cumin seeds
- Paprika
- Fenugreek
- Garam masala

Toss everything together in olive oil, then stir through a tin of heated black beans. This is tasty with wholegrain rice, to fill pittas or to have with fajitas.

Roasted Garlic, Red Onions and Brussel Sprouts – Diversity score: 10

Sprouts are not just for Christmas! They are delicious roasted with garlic and red onions, tossed in olive oil and harissa spices. I make a spice mix with equal quantities of powdered chilli, paprika, cumin, caraway seeds, ground coriander and oregano.

Once they're cooked through (they usually take around 25 minutes at 180 °C), they can be mixed with quinoa.

Vegetable and Bean Chilli – Diversity score: 10

- 1 onion, chopped
- 4 cloves of garlic, sliced
- 1 red pepper, chopped
- 1 orange pepper, chopped
- 1 tin of kidney beans
- 1 tin of butter beans
- 1 tin of chopped tomatoes
- 2 teaspoons of powdered smoked paprika
- 2 teaspoons of chilli powder (or more if you like it hot!)

Gently sauté the vegetables before adding the beans and tomatoes. Thoroughly heat through and serve with brown rice.

Vegetable Moroccan Tagine – Diversity score: 15

- 1 onion, chopped
- 4 cloves of garlic, sliced
- 2 leeks, sliced
- 1 red pepper, chopped
- 1 yellow pepper, chopped
- 1 courgette, sliced
- 1 aubergine, chopped

- 5 dried apricots, each cut in half
- 5 pitted prunes, each cut in half
- 1 tin of chopped tomatoes
- 1 tin of chickpeas
- 2 teaspoons of cinnamon
- 2 teaspoons of ground coriander
- 2 teaspoons of cumin
- 2 teaspoons of ground ginger
- 2 teaspoons of turmeric

Gently sauté the vegetables before adding the chickpeas and tomatoes. Thoroughly heat through and serve with couscous.

Quick and Easy Pasta – Diversity score: 5
- 1 red onion, chopped
- 4 cloves of garlic, sliced
- Half a punnet of closed cap mushrooms, sliced
- Half a punnet of portobello mushrooms (or any other variety of your choice), sliced
- 2 tablespoons of cream cheese
- 1 tablespoon of nutritional yeast
- 1 teaspoon of oregano

Gently sauté the vegetables before adding the cream cheese, nutritional yeast and oregano. Thoroughly heat through and serve with lentil pasta.

Mixed Vegetable Curry – Diversity score: 13
- 1 onion, chopped
- 4 cloves of garlic, sliced
- 1 butternut squash, peeled and chopped
- 1 courgette, sliced
- 1 red pepper, chopped

- 1 leek, sliced
- 1 aubergine, chopped
- 1 tin of chopped tomatoes
- A thumb-sized piece of ginger, grated
- A handful of fresh coriander
- 2 teaspoons of turmeric
- 2 teaspoons of cumin

Gently sauté the vegetables before adding the tomatoes and spices. Thoroughly heat through and serve with brown pasta.

Red and Green Pasta – Diversity score: 4

Avocado pesto:

- Blitz together 1 avocado, 2 handfuls of fresh basil, 1 tablespoon of pine nuts. Add enough olive oil to loosen the mixture to a pesto-like consistency. The pesto is also tasty if you add spinach as well.

Mix it through cooked green lentil pasta and add a handful of chopped sundried tomatoes.

Bean and Lentil Chilli – Diversity score: 14

- 1 onion, chopped
- 4 cloves of garlic, sliced
- 1 red pepper, chopped
- 1 orange pepper, chopped
- 1 yellow pepper, chopped
- 1 courgette, sliced
- 3 sticks of celery, sliced
- 1 tin of kidney beans
- 1 tin of black beans
- 1 tin of butter beans
- 1 tin of chopped tomatoes

- 2 teaspoons of sumac
- 2 teaspoons of cayenne pepper
- 2 teaspoons of chilli powder

Gently sauté the vegetables before adding the tomatoes, beans and spices. Thoroughly heat through and serve with brown rice.

10-Minute Creamy Curry – Diversity score: 9

- 1 onion, chopped
- 1 block of tofu
- A thumb-size piece of ginger, grated
- 2 teaspoons of ground coriander
- 2 teaspoons of turmeric
- 2 teaspoons of ground cumin
- 1 tin of coconut milk
- 1 tin of chickpeas
- 1 tin of cannellini beans
- 1 tablespoon of tomato purée

Chop the onion and tofu, and briefly fry in olive oil. Add the spices, coconut milk, beans and tomato purée and simmer for 10 minutes. Serve with brown rice.

Veggie Pasta Sauce – Diversity score: 9

- 1 onion, chopped
- 4 cloves of garlic, sliced
- 1 red pepper, chopped
- 1 orange pepper, chopped
- 1 courgette, sliced
- 1 broccoli, chopped
- 1 packet of passata
- 2 teaspoons of dried basil

- 2 teaspoons of dried oregano

Gently sauté the vegetables before adding the passata and herbs. Thoroughly heat through and serve with wholegrain or lentil pasta.

Asian Stir Fry – Diversity score: 7

- 8 baby sweetcorn, sliced
- 8 spears of asparagus, cut into 2cm slices
- 1 red pepper, sliced
- Purple sprouting broccoli
- 3 tablespoons of soya beans
- 2 tablespoons of soy sauce
- 1 tablespoon of peanut butter
- 2 tablespoons of tahini

Stir fry the vegetables in olive oil. Blitz together the soy sauce, peanut butter and tahini to make the sauce. Stir the sauce through the vegetables. Serve with brown rice.

Honey Vegetable Tray Bake – Diversity score: 8

- 1 cauliflower, chopped
- 3 carrots, sliced
- 2 leeks, sliced
- 1 punnet of cherry tomatoes
- 1 courgette, sliced

Marinade the chopped vegetables in a sauce made from:

- 2 tablespoons of honey
- 2 tablespoons of soy sauce
- 2 tablespoons of olive oil
- 2 teaspoons of cumin
- 2 teaspoons of turmeric

Roast at 180°C for approximately 30 minutes. Serve with quinoa.

3-Ingredient Beetroot Risotto – Diversity score: 3

- 2 beetroots
- 1 tin of coconut milk

Roast the beetroots for 40 minutes at 160ºC. Once they are soft, peel and blitz with the coconut milk. Stir through giant wholegrain couscous and serve with baby sweetcorn and green beans.

Tofu and Miso Broth – Diversity score: 3

- 1 block of tofu
- 1 red pepper, sliced
- Chopped broccoli
- Miso paste

Make a miso broth by mixing miso paste with boiling water. Add the chopped tofu and vegetables, and microwave for 2 minutes. Top with peanuts.

Side Dishes and Desserts

Green Side Salad – Diversity score: 10
- Mixed salad leaves – a typical bag includes red radicchio, delicate lamb's lettuce and crispy frisée.
- Chopped celery
- Chopped cherry tomatoes
- Green olives
- Black olives
- Chopped avocado
- Sliced gherkin
- Pine nuts

Summer Salad – Diversity score: 4
- Cook a serving of quinoa

Once it has cooled, mix through:
- 1 tablespoon of edamame beans
- 1 chopped yellow pepper
- 1 grated carrot

Pour over soy sauce to taste.

Tomato Salsa – Diversity score: 4
- Cherry tomatoes, chopped
- Finely chopped red onion
- Chopped coriander
- Lime juice

Quick Guacamole – Diversity score: 3
- 1 avocado
- At least 1 clove of garlic, crushed

- The juice of half a lemon

Mash together with a fork.

Hummus 5 Ways – Diversity score: 5 for the base

Dr Collette Stadler

The base:

- 1 tin of chickpeas*
- Half a lemon, juiced
- Olive oil
- Half a clove of garlic
- 1 tablespoon of tahini pasta
- Salt and pepper to taste
- 1 teaspoon of cumin

Drain the tin of chickpeas but keep the liquid to one side. Add to a food processor the chickpeas, garlic, lemon, a glug of olive oil, the tahini, 100ml of chickpea water, salt and pepper. Blend until smooth. If you prefer a thin consistency, add more of the chickpea water. If you enjoy the base without any extra flavours, add the cumin at this stage. If you'd like to personalise the recipe, you could try:

- Lemon zest and coriander
- Paprika and a pinch of chilli flakes
- Red pepper – finely chopped and blended into the hummus at stage 2.
- Mint and pea – handful of frozen or cooked peas added at stage 2.

*You can replace the chickpeas with cannellini beans or use 50/50 chickpeas and cannellini beans for variation.

Prune Smoothie Dessert Bowl – Diversity score: 3
- 8 prunes, seeds removed
- 2 tablespoons of oats
- 2 tablespoons of Greek yoghurt
- Add enough almond milk to create a thick, smooth consistency.

Blitz together and leave in the fridge overnight. Top with pomegranate seeds for a delicious dessert!

Chocolate Pudding – Diversity score: 3
- Blitz together 1 avocado and 2 teaspoons of raw cacao powder.

Top with blueberries.

Caramel Banana Ice Cream – Diversity score: 3
- Blitz together 1 banana, 4 pitted Medjool dates and a teaspoon of cashew butter.

Freeze for a yummy treat!

Energise your Intestinal Ecosystem!

I have previously written about using the acronym ENERGISE™ to think about ways we can modify our lifestyle to improve our health and well-being. ENERGISE™ stands for:

- Exercise and movement
- Nutrition
- Environment
- Relationships and social connections
- Goal setting
- Ideas, mindset and stress reduction
- Sleep
- Empower

I also use the same acronym to summarise the strategies we can use to nourish our healthy gut bacteria, although there are a few small changes:

- Exercise
- Nutrition
- Eat within a specific time window
- Reduce stress

- Get outside and spend time in natural environments
- Inhibit your intake of ultra-processed foods
- Sleep
- Enhance and nurture social connections

Focus on:

- Fibre
- Diversity
- Fermented foods and drinks
- Polyphenols

I really hope you've enjoyed reading this book and learning more about our amazing gut bacteria and the tremendous roles they play in health and well-being. Please get in touch if you have any questions at all! I'd love to hear from you.

Emma
@dr_emmashort

References

Al-Ghezi ZZ, Busbee PB, Alghetaa H, Nagarkatti PS, Nagarkatti M. Combination of cannabinoids, delta-9-tetrahydrocannabinol (THC) and cannabidiol (CBD), mitigates experimental autoimmune encephalomyelitis (EAE) by altering the gut microbiome. Brain Behav Immun. 2019 Nov;82:25-35. doi: 10.1016/j.bbi.2019.07.028. Epub 2019 Jul 26. PMID: 31356922; PMCID: PMC6866665.

Allen JM, Mailing LJ, Niemiro GM, Moore R, Cook MD, White BA, Holscher HD, Woods JA. Exercise Alters Gut Microbiota Composition and Function in Lean and Obese Humans. Med Sci Sports Exerc. 2018 Apr;50(4):747-757. doi: 10.1249/MSS.0000000000001495. PMID: 29166320.

Almeida A, Mitchell AL, Boland M, Forster SC, Gloor GB, Tarkowska A, Lawley TD, Finn RD. A new genomic blueprint of the human gut microbiota. Nature. 2019 Apr;568(7753):499-504. doi: 10.1038/s41586-019-0965-1. Epub 2019 Feb 11. PMID: 30745586; PMCID: PMC6784870.

Antinozzi M, Giffi M, Sini N, Gallè F, Valeriani F, De Vito C, Liguori G, Romano Spica V, Cattaruzza MS. Cigarette Smoking and Human Gut Microbiota in Healthy Adults: A

Systematic Review. Biomedicines. 2022 Feb 21;10(2):510. doi: 10.3390/biomedicines10020510. PMID: 35203720; PMCID: PMC8962244.

Arora T, Sharma R, Frost G. Propionate. Anti-obesity and satiety enhancing factor? Appetite. 2011 Apr;56(2):511-5. doi: 10.1016/j. appet.2011.01.016. Epub 2011 Jan 19. PMID: 21255628.

Aslam H, Marx W, Rocks T, Loughman A, Chandrasekaran V, Ruusunen A, Dawson SL, West M, Mullarkey E, Pasco JA, Jacka FN. The effects of dairy and dairy derivatives on the gut microbiota: a systematic literature review. Gut Microbes. 2020 Nov 9;12(1):1799533. doi: 10.1080/19490976.2020.1799533. PMID: 32835617; PMCID: PMC7524346.

Bäckhed F, Ley RE, Sonnenburg JL, Peterson DA, Gordon JI. Host-bacterial mutualism in the human intestine. Science. 2005 Mar 25;307(5717):1915-20. doi: 10.1126/science.1104816. PMID: 15790844.

Bai X, Wei H, Liu W, Coker OO, Gou H, Liu C, Zhao L, Li C, Zhou Y, Wang G, Kang W, Ng EK, Yu J. Cigarette smoke promotes colorectal cancer through modulation of gut microbiota and related metabolites. Gut. 2022 Dec;71(12):2439-2450. doi: 10.1136/gutjnl-2021-325021. Epub 2022 Apr 6. PMID: 35387878; PMCID: PMC9664112.

Bajaj JS. Alcohol, liver disease and the gut microbiota. Nat Rev Gastroenterol Hepatol. 2019 Apr;16(4):235-246. doi: 10.1038/s41575-018-0099-1. PMID: 30643227.

Baker JM, Al-Nakkash L, Herbst-Kralovetz MM. Estrogen-gut microbiome axis: Physiological and clinical implications. Maturitas.

2017 Sep;103:45-53. doi: 10.1016/j.maturitas.2017.06.025. Epub 2017 Jun 23. PMID: 28778332.

Barton W, Penney NC, Cronin O, Garcia-Perez I, Molloy MG, Holmes E, Shanahan F, Cotter PD, O'Sullivan O. The microbiome of professional athletes differs from that of more sedentary subjects in composition and particularly at the functional metabolic level. Gut. 2018 Apr;67(4):625-633. doi: 10.1136/gutjnl-2016-313627. Epub 2017 Mar 30. PMID: 28360096.

Becker SL, Manson JE. Menopause, the gut microbiome, and weight gain: correlation or causation? Menopause. 2020 Nov 23;28(3):327-331. doi: 10.1097/GME.0000000000001702. PMID: 33235036.

Bhattacharjee D, Flores C, Woelfel-Monsivais C, Seekatz AM. Diversity and Prevalence of Clostridium innocuum in the Human Gut Microbiota. mSphere. 2023 Feb 21;8(1):e0056922. doi: 10.1128/msphere.00569-22. Epub 2022 Dec 21. PMID: 36541771; PMCID: PMC9942572

Bishehsari F, Magno E, Swanson G, Desai V, Voigt RM, Forsyth CB, Keshavarzian A. Alcohol and Gut-Derived Inflammation. Alcohol Res. 2017;38(2):163-171. PMID: 28988571; PMCID: PMC5513683.

Bull MJ, Plummer NT. Part 1: The Human Gut Microbiome in Health and Disease. Integr Med (Encinitas). 2014 Dec;13(6):17-22. PMID: 26770121; PMCID: PMC4566439.

Burokas A, Arboleya S, Moloney RD, Peterson VL, Murphy K, Clarke G, Stanton C, Dinan TG, Cryan JF. Targeting the Microbiota-Gut-Brain Axis: Prebiotics Have Anxiolytic and Antidepressant-like Effects and Reverse the Impact of Chronic Stress in Mice.

Biol Psychiatry. 2017 Oct 1;82(7):472-487. doi: 10.1016/j.biopsych.2016.12.031. Epub 2017 Feb 24. PMID: 28242013.

Butler MI, Mörkl S, Sandhu KV, Cryan JF, Dinan TG. The Gut Microbiome and Mental Health: What Should We Tell Our Patients?: Le microbiote Intestinal et la Santé Mentale : que Devrions-Nous dire à nos Patients? Can J Psychiatry. 2019 Nov;64(11):747-760. doi: 10.1177/0706743719874168. Epub 2019 Sep 17. PMID: 31530002; PMCID: PMC6882070.

Bycura D, Santos AC, Shiffer A, Kyman S, Winfree K, Sutliffe J, Pearson T, Sonderegger D, Cope E, Caporaso JG. Impact of Different Exercise Modalities on the Human Gut Microbiome. Sports (Basel). 2021 Jan 21;9(2):14. doi: 10.3390/sports9020014. PMID: 33494210; PMCID: PMC7909775.

Cai J, Chen Z, Wu W, Lin Q, Liang Y. High animal protein diet and gut microbiota in human health. Crit Rev Food Sci Nutr. 2022;62(22):6225-6237. doi: 10.1080/10408398.2021.1898336. Epub 2021 Mar 16. PMID: 33724115.

Cammarota G, Masucci L, Ianiro G, Bibbò S, Dinoi G, Costamagna G, Sanguinetti M, Gasbarrini A. Randomised clinical trial: faecal microbiota transplantation by colonoscopy vs. vancomycin for the treatment of recurrent Clostridium difficile infection. Aliment Pharmacol Ther. 2015 May;41(9):835-43. doi: 10.1111/apt.13144. Epub 2015 Mar 1. PMID: 25728808.

Carabotti M, Scirocco A, Maselli MA, Severi C. The gut-brain axis: interactions between enteric microbiota, central and enteric nervous systems. Ann Gastroenterol. 2015 Apr-Jun;28(2):203-209. PMID: 25830558; PMCID: PMC4367209.

Cheng M, Ning K. Stereotypes About Enterotype: the Old and New Ideas. Genomics Proteomics Bioinformatics. 2019 Feb;17(1):4-12. doi: 10.1016/j.gpb.2018.02.004. Epub 2019 Apr 23. PMID: 31026581; PMCID: PMC6521238.

Chen KL, Madak-Erdogan Z. Estrogen and Microbiota Crosstalk: Should We Pay Attention? Trends Endocrinol Metab. 2016 Nov;27(11):752-755. doi: 10.1016/j.tem.2016.08.001. Epub 2016 Aug 20. PMID: 27553057.

Cheng D, Xie MZ. A review of a potential and promising probiotic candidate-Akkermansia muciniphila. J Appl Microbiol. 2021 Jun;130(6):1813-1822. doi: 10.1111/jam.14911. Epub 2020 Nov 15. PMID: 33113228

Chevalier G, Siopi E, Guenin-Macé L, Pascal M, Laval T, Rifflet A, Boneca IG, Demangel C, Colsch B, Pruvost A, Chu-Van E, Messager A, Leulier F, Lepousez G, Eberl G, Lledo PM. Effect of gut microbiota on depressive-like behaviors in mice is mediated by the endocannabinoid system. Nat Commun. 2020 Dec 11;11(1):6363. doi: 10.1038/s41467-020-19931-2. PMID: 33311466; PMCID: PMC7732982.

Chong HX, Yusoff NAA, Hor YY, Lew LC, Jaafar MH, Choi SB, Yusoff MSB, Wahid N, Abdullah MFIL, Zakaria N, Ong KL, Park YH, Liong MT. *Lactobacillus plantarum* DR7 alleviates stress and anxiety in adults: a randomised, double-blind, placebo-controlled study. Benef Microbes. 2019 Apr 19;10(4):355-373. doi: 10.3920/BM2018.0135. Epub 2019 Mar 18. PMID: 30882244.

Chopra K, Kumar B, Kuhad A. Pathobiological targets of depression. Expert Opin Ther Targets. 2011 Apr;15(4):379-400. doi: 10.1517/14728222.2011.553603. Epub 2011 Jan 23. PMID: 21254923.

Cignarella F, Cantoni C, Ghezzi L, Salter A, Dorsett Y, Chen L, Phillips D, Weinstock GM, Fontana L, Cross AH, Zhou Y, Piccio L. Intermittent Fasting Confers Protection in CNS Autoimmunity by Altering the Gut Microbiota. Cell Metab. 2018 Jun 5;27(6):1222-1235.e6. doi: 10.1016/j.cmet.2018.05.006. PMID: 29874567; PMCID: PMC6460288.

Clapp M, Aurora N, Herrera L, Bhatia M, Wilen E, Wakefield S. Gut microbiota's effect on mental health: The gut-brain axis. Clin Pract. 2017 Sep 15;7(4):987. doi: 10.4081/cp.2017.987. PMID: 29071061; PMCID: PMC5641835.

Clauss M, Gérard P, Mosca A, Leclerc M. Interplay Between Exercise and Gut Microbiome in the Context of Human Health and Performance. Front Nutr. 2021 Jun 10;8:637010. doi: 10.3389/fnut.2021.637010. PMID: 34179053; PMCID: PMC8222532.

Cluny NL, Keenan CM, Reimer RA, Le Foll B, Sharkey KA. Prevention of Diet-Induced Obesity Effects on Body Weight and Gut Microbiota in Mice Treated Chronically with Δ9-Tetrahydrocannabinol. PLoS One. 2015 Dec 3;10(12):e0144270. doi: 10.1371/journal.pone.0144270. PMID: 26633823; PMCID: PMC4669115.

Dehhaghi M, Kazemi Shariat Panahi H, Guillemin GJ. Microorganisms, Tryptophan Metabolism, and Kynurenine Pathway: A Complex Interconnected Loop Influencing Human Health Status. Int J Tryptophan Res. 2019 Jun 19;12:1178646919852996. doi: 10.1177/1178646919852996. PMID: 31258331; PMCID: PMC6585246.

Dempsey E, Corr SC. Lactobacillus spp. for Gastrointestinal Health: Current and Future Perspectives. Front Immunol. 2022 Apr

6;13:840245. doi: 10.3389/fimmu.2022.840245. PMID: 35464397; PMCID: PMC9019120

Derrien M, van Hylckama Vlieg JE. Fate, activity, and impact of ingested bacteria within the human gut microbiota. Trends Microbiol. 2015 Jun;23(6):354-66. doi: 10.1016/j.tim.2015.03.002. Epub 2015 Apr 1. PMID: 25840765.

Diaz Heijtz R, Wang S, Anuar F, Qian Y, Björkholm B, Samuelsson A, Hibberd ML, Forssberg H, Pettersson S. Normal gut microbiota modulates brain development and behavior. Proc Natl Acad Sci U S A. 2011 Feb 15;108(7):3047-52. doi: 10.1073/pnas.1010529108. Epub 2011 Jan 31. PMID: 21282636; PMCID: PMC3041077.

Diether NE, Willing BP. Microbial Fermentation of Dietary Protein: An Important Factor in Diet☐Microbe☒Host Interaction. Microorganisms. 2019 Jan 13;7(1):19. doi: 10.3390/microorganisms7010019. PMID: 30642098; PMCID: PMC6352118.

Dill-McFarland KA, Tang ZZ, Kemis JH, Kerby RL, Chen G, Palloni A, Sorenson T, Rey FE, Herd P. Close social relationships correlate with human gut microbiota composition. Sci Rep. 2019 Jan 24;9(1):703. doi: 10.1038/s41598-018-37298-9. PMID: 30679677; PMCID: PMC6345772.

Di Pierro F. A Possible Perspective about the Compositional Models, Evolution, and Clinical Meaning of Human Enterotypes. Microorganisms. 2021 Nov 12;9(11):2341. doi: 10.3390/microorganisms9112341. PMID: 34835466; PMCID: PMC8618122.

Dubin K, Pamer EG. Enterococci and Their Interactions with the Intestinal Microbiome. Microbiol Spectr. 2014 Nov;5(6):10.1128/

microbiolspec.BAD-0014-2016. doi: 10.1128/microbiolspec.BAD-0014-2016. PMID: 29125098; PMCID: PMC5691600.

Durack J, Kimes NE, Lin DL, Rauch M, McKean M, McCauley K, Panzer AR, Mar JS, Cabana MD, Lynch SV. Delayed gut microbiota development in high-risk for asthma infants is temporarily modifiable by Lactobacillus supplementation. Nat Commun. 2018 Feb 16;9(1):707. doi: 10.1038/s41467-018-03157-4. PMID: 29453431; PMCID: PMC5816017.

Durk RP, Castillo E, Márquez-Magaña L, Grosicki GJ, Bolter ND, Lee CM, Bagley JR. Gut Microbiota Composition Is Related to Cardiorespiratory Fitness in Healthy Young Adults. Int J Sport Nutr Exerc Metab. 2019 May 1;29(3):249-253. doi: 10.1123/ijsnem.2018-0024. Epub 2018 Oct 28. PMID: 29989465; PMCID: PMC6487229.

Ejtahed HS, Hasani-Ranjbar S, Siadat SD, Larijani B. The most important challenges ahead of microbiome pattern in the post era of the COVID-19 pandemic. J Diabetes Metab Disord. 2020 Jul 3;19(2):2031-2033. doi: 10.1007/s40200-020-00579-0. PMID: 32837956; PMCID: PMC7332307.

Elvers KT, Wilson VJ, Hammond A, Duncan L, Huntley AL, Hay AD, van der Werf ET. Antibiotic-induced changes in the human gut microbiota for the most commonly prescribed antibiotics in primary care in the UK: a systematic review. BMJ Open. 2020 Sep 21;10(9):e035677. doi: 10.1136/bmjopen-2019-035677. PMID: 32958481; PMCID: PMC7507860.

Engen PA, Green SJ, Voigt RM, Forsyth CB, Keshavarzian A. The Gastrointestinal Microbiome: Alcohol Effects on the Composition of Intestinal Microbiota. Alcohol Res. 2015;37(2):223-36. PMID: 26695747; PMCID: PMC4590619.

Fernández-Alonso M, Aguirre Camorlinga A, Messiah SE, Marroquin E. Effect of adding probiotics to an antibiotic intervention on the human gut microbial diversity and composition: a systematic review. J Med Microbiol. 2022 Nov;71(11). doi: 10.1099/jmm.0.001625. PMID: 36382780.

Ferreira-Halder CV, Faria AVS, Andrade SS. Action and function of Faecalibacterium prausnitzii in health and disease. Best Pract Res Clin Gastroenterol. 2017 Dec;31(6):643-648. doi: 10.1016/j.bpg.2017.09.011. Epub 2017 Sep 18. PMID: 29566907.

Flint HJ. The impact of nutrition on the human microbiome. Nutr Rev. 2012 Aug;70 Suppl 1:S10-3. doi: 10.1111/j.1753-4887.2012.00499.x. PMID: 22861801.

Goodrich JK, Waters JL, Poole AC, Sutter JL, Koren O, Blekhman R, Beaumont M, Van Treuren W, Knight R, Bell JT, Spector TD, Clark AG, Ley RE. Human genetics shape the gut microbiome. Cell. 2014 Nov 6;159(4):789-99. doi: 10.1016/j.cell.2014.09.053. PMID: 25417156; PMCID: PMC4255478.

Green J, Castle D, Berk M, Hair C, Loughman A, Cryan J, Nierenberg A, Athan E, Jacka F. Faecal microbiota transplants for depression – Who gives a crapsule? Aust N Z J Psychiatry. 2019 Aug;53(8):732-734. doi: 10.1177/0004867419839776. Epub 2019 Apr 8. PMID: 30957511.

Gui X, Yang Z, Li MD. Effect of Cigarette Smoke on Gut Microbiota: State of Knowledge. Front Physiol. 2021 Jun 17;12:673341. doi: 10.3389/fphys.2021.673341. PMID: 34220536; PMCID: PMC8245763.

Guo P, Zhang K, Ma X, He P. *Clostridium* species as probiotics: potentials and challenges. J Anim Sci Biotechnol. 2020 Feb

20;11:24. doi: 10.1186/s40104-019-0402-1. PMID: 32099648; PMCID: PMC7031906.

Hill C, Guarner F, Reid G, Gibson GR, Merenstein DJ, Pot B, Morelli L, Canani RB, Flint HJ, Salminen S, Calder PC, Sanders ME. Expert consensus document. The International Scientific Association for Probiotics and Prebiotics consensus statement on the scope and appropriate use of the term probiotic. Nat Rev Gastroenterol Hepatol. 2014 Aug;11(8):506-14. doi: 10.1038/ nrgastro.2014.66. Epub 2014 Jun 10. PMID: 24912386.

InformedHealth.org [Internet]. Cologne, Germany: Institute for Quality and Efficiency in Health Care (IQWiG); 2006-. Depression: How effective are antidepressants? [Updated 2020 Jun 18]. Available from: https://www.ncbi.nlm.nih.gov/books/NBK361016/

Jacka FN, O'Neil A, Opie R, Itsiopoulos C, Cotton S, Mohebbi M, Castle D, Dash S, Mihalopoulos C, Chatterton ML, Brazionis L, Dean OM, Hodge AM, Berk M. A randomised controlled trial of dietary improvement for adults with major depression (the 'SMILES' trial). BMC Med. 2017 Jan 30;15(1):23. doi: 10.1186/ s12916-017-0791-y. Erratum in: BMC Med. 2018 Dec 28;16(1):236. PMID: 28137247; PMCID: PMC5282719.

Jackson MA, Verdi S, Maxan ME, Shin CM, Zierer J, Bowyer RCE, Martin T, Williams FMK, Menni C, Bell JT, Spector TD, Steves CJ. Gut microbiota associations with common diseases and prescription medications in a population-based cohort. Nat Commun. 2018 Jul 9;9(1):2655. doi: 10.1038/s41467-018-05184-7. PMID: 29985401; PMCID: PMC6037668.

Kaur CP, Vadivelu J, Chandramathi S. Impact of Klebsiella pneumoniae in lower gastrointestinal tract diseases. J Dig Dis.

2018 May;19(5):262-271. doi: 10.1111/1751-2980.12595. Epub 2018 May 20. PMID: 29573336.

Kawano Y, Edwards M, Huang Y, Bilate AM, Araujo LP, Tanoue T, Atarashi K, Ladinsky MS, Reiner SL, Wang HH, Mucida D, Honda K, Ivanov II. Microbiota imbalance induced by dietary sugar disrupts immune-mediated protection from metabolic syndrome. Cell. 2022 Sep 15;185(19):3501-3519.e20. doi: 10.1016/j.cell.2022.08.005. Epub 2022 Aug 29. PMID: 36041436; PMCID: PMC9556172.

Khan S, Waliullah S, Godfrey V, Khan MAW, Ramachandran RA, Cantarel BL, Behrendt C, Peng L, Hooper LV, Zaki H. Dietary simple sugars alter microbial ecology in the gut and promote colitis in mice. Sci Transl Med. 2020 Oct 28;12(567):eaay6218. doi: 10.1126/scitranslmed.aay6218. PMID: 33115951.

King CH, Desai H, Sylvetsky AC, LoTempio J, Ayanyan S, Carrie J, Crandall KA, Fochtman BC, Gasparyan L, Gulzar N, Howell P, Issa N, Krampis K, Mishra L, Morizono H, Pisegna JR, Rao S, Ren Y, Simonyan V, Smith K, VedBrat S, Yao MD, Mazumder R. Baseline human gut microbiota profile in healthy people and standard reporting template. PLoS One. 2019 Sep 11;14(9):e0206484. doi: 10.1371/journal.pone.0206484. PMID: 31509535; PMCID: PMC6738582.

Koh A, De Vadder F, Kovatcheva-Datchary P, Bäckhed F. From Dietary Fiber to Host Physiology: Short-Chain Fatty Acids as Key Bacterial Metabolites. Cell. 2016 Jun 2;165(6):1332-1345. doi: 10.1016/j.cell.2016.05.041. PMID: 27259147.

Kort R, Caspers M, van de Graaf A, van Egmond W, Keijser B, Roeselers G. Shaping the oral microbiota through intimate kissing.

Microbiome. 2014 Nov 17;2:41. doi: 10.1186/2049-2618-2-41. PMID: 25408893; PMCID: PMC4233210.

Kumar Singh A, Cabral C, Kumar R, Ganguly R, Kumar Rana H, Gupta A, Rosaria Lauro M, Carbone C, Reis F, Pandey AK. Beneficial Effects of Dietary Polyphenols on Gut Microbiota and Strategies to Improve Delivery Efficiency. Nutrients. 2019 Sep 13;11(9):2216. doi: 10.3390/nu11092216. PMID: 31540270; PMCID: PMC6770155.

Levan SR, Stamnes KA, Lin DL, Panzer AR, Fukui E, McCauley K, Fujimura KE, McKean M, Ownby DR, Zoratti EM, Boushey HA, Cabana MD, Johnson CC, Lynch SV. Elevated faecal 12,13-diHOME concentration in neonates at high risk for asthma is produced by gut bacteria and impedes immune tolerance. Nat Microbiol. 2019 Nov;4(11):1851-1861. doi: 10.1038/s41564-019-0498-2. Epub 2019 Jul 22. Erratum in: Nat Microbiol. 2019 Sep 6;: PMID: 31332384; PMCID: PMC6830510.

Li Y, Hao Y, Fan F, Zhang B. The Role of Microbiome in Insomnia, Circadian Disturbance and Depression. Front Psychiatry. 2018 Dec 5;9:669. doi: 10.3389/fpsyt.2018.00669. PMID: 30568608; PMCID: PMC6290721.

Lim EY, Lee SY, Shin HS, Lee J, Nam YD, Lee DO, Lee JY, Yeon SH, Son RH, Park CL, Heo YH, Kim YT. The Effect of *Lactobacillus acidophilus* YT1 (MENOLACTO) on Improving Menopausal Symptoms: A Randomized, Double-Blinded, Placebo-Controlled Clinical Trial. J Clin Med. 2020 Jul 9;9(7):2173. doi: 10.3390/jcm9072173. PMID: 32660010; PMCID: PMC7408745.

Lindstedt K, Buczek D, Pedersen T, Hjerde E, Raffelsberger N, Suzuki Y, Brisse S, Holt K, Samuelsen Ø, Sundsfjord A. Detection of

Klebsiella pneumoniae human gut carriage: a comparison of culture, qPCR, and whole metagenomic sequencing methods. Gut Microbes. 2022 Jan-Dec;14(1):2118500. doi: 10.1080/19490976.2022.2118500. PMID: 36045603; PMCID: PMC9450895.

Ljungberg T, Bondza E, Lethin C. Evidence of the Importance of Dietary Habits Regarding Depressive Symptoms and Depression. Int J Environ Res Public Health. 2020 Mar 2;17(5):1616. doi: 10.3390/ijerph17051616. PMID: 32131552; PMCID: PMC7084175.

Madison A, Kiecolt-Glaser JK. Stress, depression, diet, and the gut microbiota: human-bacteria interactions at the core of psychoneuroimmunology and nutrition. Curr Opin Behav Sci. 2019 Aug;28:105-110. doi: 10.1016/j.cobeha.2019.01.011. Epub 2019 Mar 25. PMID: 32395568; PMCID: PMC7213601.

Madsen L, Myrmel LS, Fjære E, Liaset B, Kristiansen K. Links between Dietary Protein Sources, the Gut Microbiota, and Obesity. Front Physiol. 2017 Dec 19;8:1047. doi: 10.3389/fphys.2017.01047. PMID: 29311977; PMCID: PMC5742165.

Magne F, Gotteland M, Gauthier L, Zazueta A, Pesoa S, Navarrete P, Balamurugan R. The Firmicutes/Bacteroidetes Ratio: A Relevant Marker of Gut Dysbiosis in Obese Patients? Nutrients. 2020 May 19;12(5):1474. doi: 10.3390/nu12051474. PMID: 32438689; PMCID: PMC7285218.

Maier L, Pruteanu M, Kuhn M, Zeller G, Telzerow A, Anderson EE, Brochado AR, Fernandez KC, Dose H, Mori H, Patil KR, Bork P, Typas A. Extensive impact of non-antibiotic drugs on human gut bacteria. Nature. 2018 Mar 29;555(7698):623-628. doi: 10.1038/nature25979. Epub 2018 Mar 19. PMID: 29555994; PMCID: PMC6108420.

Maifeld A, Bartolomaeus H, Löber U, Avery EG, Steckhan N, Markó L, Wilck N, Hamad I, Šušnjar U, Mähler A, Hohmann C, Chen CY, Cramer H, Dobos G, Lesker TR, Strowig T, Dechend R, Bzdok D, Kleinewietfeld M, Michalsen A, Müller DN, Forslund SK. Fasting alters the gut microbiome reducing blood pressure and body weight in metabolic syndrome patients. Nat Commun. 2021 Mar 30;12(1):1970. doi: 10.1038/s41467-021-22097-0. PMID: 33785752; PMCID: PMC8010079.

Mailing LJ, Allen JM, Buford TW, Fields CJ, Woods JA. Exercise and the Gut Microbiome: A Review of the Evidence, Potential Mechanisms, and Implications for Human Health. Exerc Sport Sci Rev. 2019 Apr;47(2):75-85. doi: 10.1249/JES.0000000000000183. PMID: 30883471.

Maioli TU, Borras-Nogues E, Torres L, Barbosa SC, Martins VD, Langella P, Azevedo VA, Chatel JM. Possible Benefits of *Faecalibacterium prausnitzii* for Obesity-Associated Gut Disorders. Front Pharmacol. 2021 Dec 2;12:740636. doi: 10.3389/fphar.2021.740636. PMID: 34925006; PMCID: PMC8677946.

Manoogian ENC, Chow LS, Taub PR, Laferrère B, Panda S. Time-restricted Eating for the Prevention and Management of Metabolic Diseases. Endocr Rev. 2022 Mar 9;43(2):405-436. doi: 10.1210/endrev/bnab027. PMID: 34550357; PMCID: PMC8905332.

Madison A, Kiecolt-Glaser JK. Stress, depression, diet, and the gut microbiota: human-bacteria interactions at the core of psychoneuroimmunology and nutrition. Curr Opin Behav Sci. 2019 Aug;28:105-110. doi: 10.1016/j.cobeha.2019.01.011. Epub 2019 Mar 25. PMID: 32395568; PMCID: PMC7213601.

Martinson JNV, Walk ST. *Escherichia coli* Residency in the Gut of Healthy Human Adults. EcoSal Plus. 2020 Sep;9(1):10.1128/ecosalplus.ESP-0003-2020. doi: 10.1128/ecosalplus.ESP-0003-2020. PMID: 32978935; PMCID: PMC7523338.

Mayneris-Perxachs J, Arnoriaga-Rodríguez M, Luque-Córdoba D, Priego-Capote F, Pérez-Brocal V, Moya A, Burokas A, Maldonado R, Fernández-Real JM. Gut microbiota steroid sexual dimorphism and its impact on gonadal steroids: influences of obesity and menopausal status. Microbiome. 2020 Sep 20;8(1):136. doi: 10.1186/s40168-020-00913-x. PMID: 32951609; PMCID: PMC7504665.

Mazier W, Le Corf K, Martinez C, Tudela H, Kissi D, Kropp C, Coubard C, Soto M, Elustondo F, Rawadi G, Claus SP. A New Strain of *Christensenella minuta* as a Potential Biotherapy for Obesity and Associated Metabolic Diseases. Cells. 2021 Apr 6;10(4):823. doi: 10.3390/cells10040823. PMID: 33917566; PMCID: PMC8067450.

McDonald D, Hyde E, Debelius JW, Morton JT, Gonzalez A, Ackermann G, Aksenov AA, Behsaz B, Brennan C, Chen Y, DeRight Goldasich L, Dorrestein PC, Dunn RR, Fahimipour AK, Gaffney J, Gilbert JA, Gogul G, Green JL, Hugenholtz P, Humphrey G, Huttenhower C, Jackson MA, Janssen S, Jeste DV, Jiang L, Kelley ST, Knights D, Kosciolek T, Ladau J, Leach J, Marotz C, Meleshko D, Melnik AV, Metcalf JL, Mohimani H, Montassier E, Navas-Molina J, Nguyen TT, Peddada S, Pevzner P, Pollard KS, Rahnavard G, Robbins-Pianka A, Sangwan N, Shorenstein J, Smarr L, Song SJ, Spector T, Swafford AD, Thackray VG, Thompson LR, Tripathi A, Vázquez-Baeza Y, Vrbanac A, Wischmeyer P, Wolfe E, Zhu Q; American Gut Consortium; Knight R. American Gut: an Open Platform for Citizen Science Microbiome Research. mSystems. 2018 May 15;3(3):e00031-18.

doi: 10.1128/mSystems.00031-18. PMID: 29795809; PMCID: PMC5954204.

Menni C, Jackson MA, Pallister T, Steves CJ, Spector TD, Valdes AM. Gut microbiome diversity and high-fibre intake are related to lower long-term weight gain. Int J Obes (Lond). 2017 Jul;41(7):1099-1105. doi: 10.1038/ijo.2017.66. Epub 2017 Mar 13. PMID: 28286339; PMCID: PMC5500185.

Meroni M, Longo M, Dongiovanni P. Alcohol or Gut Microbiota: Who Is the Guilty? Int J Mol Sci. 2019 Sep 14;20(18):4568. doi: 10.3390/ijms20184568. PMID: 31540133; PMCID: PMC6770333.

Monda V, Villano I, Messina A, Valenzano A, Esposito T, Moscatelli F, Viggiano A, Cibelli G, Chieffi S, Monda M, Messina G. Exercise Modifies the Gut Microbiota with Positive Health Effects. Oxid Med Cell Longev. 2017;2017:3831972. doi: 10.1155/2017/3831972. Epub 2017 Mar 5. PMID: 28357027; PMCID: PMC5357536.

Mörkl S, Butler MI, Lackner S. Advances in the gut microbiome and mood disorders. Curr Opin Psychiatry. 2023 Jan 1;36(1):1-7. doi: 10.1097/YCO.0000000000000829. PMID: 36131643.

Mousavi SN, Rayyani E, Heshmati J, Tavasolian R, Rahimlou M. Effects of Ramadan and Non-ramadan Intermittent Fasting on Gut Microbiome. Front Nutr. 2022 Mar 22;9:860575. doi: 10.3389/fnut.2022.860575. PMID: 35392284; PMCID: PMC8980861.

Nash V, Ranadheera CS, Georgousopoulou EN, Mellor DD, Panagiotakos DB, McKune AJ, Kellett J, Naumovski N. The effects of grape and red wine polyphenols on gut microbiota – A systematic review. Food Res Int. 2018 Nov;113:277-287. doi: 10.1016/j.foodres.2018.07.019. Epub 2018 Jul 11. PMID: 30195522.

Ndongo S, Armstrong N, Raoult D, Fournier PE. Reclassification of eight Akkermansia muciniphila strains and description of Akkermansia massiliensis sp. nov. and Candidatus Akkermansia timonensis, isolated from human feces. Sci Rep. 2022 Dec 16;12(1):21747. doi: 10.1038/s41598-022-25873-0. PMID: 36526682; PMCID: PMC9758162.

Neroni B, Evangelisti M, Radocchia G, Di Nardo G, Pantanella F, Villa MP, Schippa S. Relationship between sleep disorders and gut dysbiosis: what affects what? Sleep Med. 2021 Nov;87:1-7. doi: 10.1016/j.sleep.2021.08.003. Epub 2021 Aug 18. PMID: 34479058.

Nguyen TT, Zhang X, Wu TC, Liu J, Le C, Tu XM, Knight R, Jeste DV. Association of Loneliness and Wisdom With Gut Microbial Diversity and Composition: An Exploratory Study. Front Psychiatry. 2021 Mar 25;12:648475. doi: 10.3389/fpsyt.2021.648475. PMID: 33841213; PMCID: PMC8029068.

Nishida K, Sawada D, Kuwano Y, Tanaka H, Sugawara T, Aoki Y, Fujiwara S, Rokutan K. Daily administration of paraprobiotic Lactobacillus gasseri CP2305 ameliorates chronic stress-associated symptoms in Japanese medical students. Journal of Functional Foods. 2017; 36:112-121. ISSN 1756-4646.

Nurminen N, Lin J, Grönroos M, Puhakka R, Kramna L, Vari HK, Viskari H, Oikarinen S, Roslund M, Parajuli A, Tyni I, Cinek O, Laitinen O, Hyöty H, Sinkkonen A. Nature-derived microbiota exposure as a novel immunomodulatory approach. Future Microbiol. 2018 Jun 1;13:737-744. doi: 10.2217/fmb-2017-0286. Epub 2018 May 17. PMID: 29771153.

Pandey KB, Rizvi SI. Plant polyphenols as dietary antioxidants in human health and disease. Oxid Med Cell Longev. 2009 Nov-

Dec;2(5):270-8. doi: 10.4161/oxim.2.5.9498. PMID: 20716914; PMCID: PMC2835915.

Panduro A, Rivera-Iñiguez I, Sepulveda-Villegas M, Roman S. Genes, emotions and gut microbiota: The next frontier for the gastroenterologist. World J Gastroenterol. 2017 May 7;23(17):3030-3042. doi: 10.3748/wjg.v23.i17.3030. PMID: 28533660; PMCID: PMC5423040.

Panee J, Gerschenson M, Chang L. Associations Between Microbiota, Mitochondrial Function, and Cognition in Chronic Marijuana Users. J Neuroimmune Pharmacol. 2018 Mar;13(1):113-122. doi: 10.1007/s11481-017-9767-0. Epub 2017 Nov 4. PMID: 29101632; PMCID: PMC5790619.

Parajuli A, Hui N, Puhakka R, Oikarinen S, Grönroos M, Selonen VAO, Siter N, Kramna L, Roslund MI, Vari HK, Nurminen N, Honkanen H, Hintikka J, Sarkkinen H, Romantschuk M, Kauppi M, Valve R, Cinek O, Laitinen OH, Rajaniemi J, Hyöty H, Sinkkonen A; ADELE study group (all additional members of the ADELE study group in Lahti and Tampere). Yard vegetation is associated with gut microbiota composition. Sci Total Environ. 2020 Apr 15;713:136707. doi: 10.1016/j.scitotenv.2020.136707. Epub 2020 Jan 15. PMID: 32019041.

Peters BA, Santoro N, Kaplan RC, Qi Q. Spotlight on the Gut Microbiome in Menopause: Current Insights. Int J Womens Health. 2022 Aug 10;14:1059-1072. doi: 10.2147/IJWH.S340491. PMID: 35983178; PMCID: PMC9379122.

Rao AV, Bested AC, Beaulne TM, Katzman MA, Iorio C, Berardi JM, Logan AC. A randomized, double-blind, placebo-controlled pilot study of a probiotic in emotional symptoms of chronic fatigue syndrome. Gut Pathog. 2009 Mar 19;1(1):6. doi: 10.1186/1757-4749-1-6. PMID: 19338686; PMCID: PMC2664325.

Ramirez J, Guarner F, Bustos Fernandez L, Maruy A, Sdepanian VL, Cohen H. Antibiotics as Major Disruptors of Gut Microbiota. Front Cell Infect Microbiol. 2020 Nov 24;10:572912. doi: 10.3389/fcimb.2020.572912. PMID: 33330122; PMCID: PMC7732679.

Rashid MU, Zaura E, Buijs MJ, Keijser BJ, Crielaard W, Nord CE, Weintraub A. Determining the Long-term Effect of Antibiotic Administration on the Human Normal Intestinal Microbiota Using Culture and Pyrosequencing Methods. Clin Infect Dis. 2015 May 15;60 Suppl 2:S77-84. doi: 10.1093/cid/civ137. PMID: 25922405.

Ridaura VK, Faith JJ, Rey FE, Cheng J, Duncan AE, Kau AL, Griffin NW, Lombard V, Henrissat B, Bain JR, Muehlbauer MJ, Ilkayeva O, Semenkovich CF, Funai K, Hayashi DK, Lyle BJ, Martini MC, Ursell LK, Clemente JC, Van Treuren W, Walters WA, Knight R, Newgard CB, Heath AC, Gordon JI. Gut microbiota from twins discordant for obesity modulate metabolism in mice. Science. 2013 Sep 6;341(6150):1241214. doi: 10.1126/science.1241214. PMID: 24009397; PMCID: PMC3829625.

Rogers MAM, Aronoff DM. The influence of non-steroidal anti-inflammatory drugs on the gut microbiome. Clin Microbiol Infect. 2016 Feb;22(2):178.e1-178.e9. doi: 10.1016/j.cmi.2015.10.003. Epub 2015 Oct 16. PMID: 26482265; PMCID: PMC4754147.

Sato M, Suzuki Y. Alterations in intestinal microbiota in ultramarathon runners. Sci Rep. 2022 Apr 28;12(1):6984. doi: 10.1038/s41598-022-10791-y. PMID: 35484386; PMCID: PMC9050700.

Sen P, Molinero-Perez A, O'Riordan KJ, McCafferty CP, O'Halloran KD, Cryan JF. Microbiota and sleep: awakening the gut feeling. Trends Mol Med. 2021 Oct;27(10):935-945. doi: 10.1016/j. molmed.2021.07.004. Epub 2021 Aug 4. PMID: 34364787.

Shreiner AB, Kao JY, Young VB. The gut microbiome in health and in disease. Curr Opin Gastroenterol. 2015 Jan;31(1):69-75. doi: 10.1097/MOG.0000000000000139. PMID: 25394236; PMCID: PMC4290017.

Shuai M, Zuo LS, Miao Z, Gou W, Xu F, Jiang Z, Ling CW, Fu Y, Xiong F, Chen YM, Zheng JS. Multi-omics analyses reveal relationships among dairy consumption, gut microbiota and cardiometabolic health. EBioMedicine. 2021 Apr;66:103284. doi: 10.1016/j.ebiom.2021.103284. Epub 2021 Mar 19. PMID: 33752125; PMCID: PMC7985282.

Silk DB, Davis A, Vulevic J, Tzortzis G, Gibson GR. Clinical trial: the effects of a trans-galactooligosaccharide prebiotic on faecal microbiota and symptoms in irritable bowel syndrome. Aliment Pharmacol Ther. 2009 Mar 1;29(5):508-18. doi: 10.1111/j.1365-2036.2008.03911.x. Epub 2008 Dec 2. PMID: 19053980.

Silva YP, Bernardi A, Frozza RL. The Role of Short-Chain Fatty Acids From Gut Microbiota in Gut-Brain Communication. Front Endocrinol (Lausanne). 2020 Jan 31;11:25. doi: 10.3389/fendo.2020.00025. PMID: 32082260; PMCID: PMC7005631.

Skinner CM, Nookaew I, Ewing LE, Wongsurawat T, Jenjaroenpun P, Quick CM, Yee EU, Piccolo BD, ElSohly M, Walker LA, Gurley B, Koturbash I. Potential Probiotic or Trigger of Gut Inflammation – The Janus-Faced Nature of Cannabidiol-Rich Cannabis Extract. J Diet Suppl. 2020;17(5):543-560. doi:

10.1080/19390211.2020.1761506. Epub 2020 May 13. PMID: 32400224; PMCID: PMC7470626.

Smith RP, Easson C, Lyle SM, Kapoor R, Donnelly CP, Davidson EJ, Parikh E, Lopez JV, Tartar JL. Gut microbiome diversity is associated with sleep physiology in humans. PLoS One. 2019 Oct 7;14(10):e0222394. doi: 10.1371/journal.pone.0222394. PMID: 31589627; PMCID: PMC6779243.

Sobko T, Liang S, Cheng WHG, Tun HM. Impact of outdoor nature-related activities on gut microbiota, fecal serotonin, and perceived stress in preschool children: the Play&Grow randomized controlled trial. Sci Rep. 2020 Dec 15;10(1):21993. doi: 10.1038/s41598-020-78642-2. PMID: 33319792; PMCID: PMC7738543.

Strandwitz P. Neurotransmitter modulation by the gut microbiota. Brain Res. 2018 Aug 15;1693(Pt B):128-133. doi: 10.1016/j.brainres.2018.03.015. PMID: 29903615; PMCID: PMC6005194.

Stojanov S, Berlec A, Štrukelj B. The Influence of Probiotics on the Firmicutes/Bacteroidetes Ratio in the Treatment of Obesity and Inflammatory Bowel disease. Microorganisms. 2020 Nov 1;8(11):1715. doi: 10.3390/microorganisms8111715. PMID: 33139627; PMCID: PMC7692443.

Su J, Wang Y, Zhang X, Ma M, Xie Z, Pan Q, Ma Z, Peppelenbosch MP. Remodeling of the gut microbiome during Ramadan-associated intermittent fasting. Am J Clin Nutr. 2021 May 8;113(5):1332-1342. doi: 10.1093/ajcn/nqaa388. PMID: 33842951; PMCID: PMC8106760.

Suez J, Korem T, Zeevi D, Zilberman-Schapira G, Thaiss CA, Maza O, Israeli D, Zmora N, Gilad S, Weinberger A, Kuperman Y,

Harmelin A, Kolodkin-Gal I, Shapiro H, Halpern Z, Segal E, Elinav E. Artificial sweeteners induce glucose intolerance by altering the gut microbiota. Nature. 2014 Oct 9;514(7521):181-6. doi: 10.1038/nature13793. Epub 2014 Sep 17. PMID: 25231862.

Suez J, Zmora N, Zilberman-Schapira G, Mor U, Dori-Bachash M, Bashiardes S, Zur M, Regev-Lehavi D, Ben-Zeev Brik R, Federici S, Horn M, Cohen Y, Moor AE, Zeevi D, Korem T, Kotler E, Harmelin A, Itzkovitz S, Maharshak N, Shibolet O, Pevsner-Fischer M, Shapiro H, Sharon I, Halpern Z, Segal E, Elinav E. Post-Antibiotic Gut Mucosal Microbiome Reconstitution Is Impaired by Probiotics and Improved by Autologous FMT. Cell. 2018 Sep 6;174(6):1406-1423.e16. doi: 10.1016/j.cell.2018.08.047. PMID: 30193113.

Swarte JC, Eelderink C, Douwes RM, Said MY, Hu S, Post A, Westerhuis R, Bakker SJL, Harmsen HJM. Effect of High versus Low Dairy Consumption on the Gut Microbiome: Results of a Randomized, Cross-Over Study. Nutrients. 2020 Jul 17;12(7):2129. doi: 10.3390/nu12072129. PMID: 32708991; PMCID: PMC7400927.

Tan J, Ni D, Taitz J, Pinget GV, Read M, Senior A, Wali JA, Elnour R, Shanahan E, Wu H, Chadban SJ, Nanan R, King NJC, Grau GE, Simpson SJ, Macia L. Dietary protein increases T-cell-independent sIgA production through changes in gut microbiota-derived extracellular vesicles. Nat Commun. 2022 Jul 27;13(1):4336. doi: 10.1038/s41467-022-31761-y. PMID: 35896537; PMCID: PMC9329401.

Tillisch K, Mayer EA, Gupta A, Gill Z, Brazeilles R, Le Nevé B, van Hylckama Vlieg JET, Guyonnet D, Derrien M, Labus JS. Brain Structure and Response to Emotional Stimuli as Related to Gut Microbial Profiles in Healthy Women. Psychosom Med. 2017

Oct;79(8):905-913. doi: 10.1097/PSY.0000000000000493. PMID: 28661940; PMCID: PMC6089374.

Toribio-Mateas MA, Bester A, Klimenko N. Impact of Plant-Based Meat Alternatives on the Gut Microbiota of Consumers: A Real-World Study. Foods. 2021 Aug 30;10(9):2040. doi: 10.3390/foods10092040. PMID: 34574149; PMCID: PMC8465665.

Valdes AM, Walter J, Segal E, Spector TD. Role of the gut microbiota in nutrition and health. BMJ. 2018 Jun 13;361:k2179. doi: 10.1136/bmj.k2179. PMID: 29899036; PMCID: PMC6000740.

Valles-Colomer M, Falony G, Darzi Y, Tigchelaar EF, Wang J, Tito RY, Schiweck C, Kurilshikov A, Joossens M, Wijmenga C, Claes S, Van Oudenhove L, Zhernakova A, Vieira-Silva S, Raes J. The neuroactive potential of the human gut microbiota in quality of life and depression. Nat Microbiol. 2019 Apr;4(4):623-632. doi: 10.1038/s41564-018-0337-x. Epub 2019 Feb 4. PMID: 30718848.

Vizioli C, Jaime-Lara R, Daniel SG, Franks A, Diallo AF, Bittinger K, Tan TP, Merenstein DJ, Brooks B, Joseph PV, Maki KA. Administration of *Bifidobacterium animalis* subsp. *lactis* Strain BB-1' in Healthy Children: Characterization, Functional Composition, and Metabolism of the Gut Microbiome. medRxiv [Preprint]. 2023 Feb 6:2023.02.02.23285145. doi: 10.1101/2023.02.02.23285145. PMID: 36798243; PMCID: PMC9934720.

Wieërs G, Belkhir L, Enaud R, Leclercq S, Philippart de Foy JM, Dequenne I, de Timary P, Cani PD. How Probiotics Affect the Microbiota. Front Cell Infect Microbiol. 2020 Jan 15;9:454. doi: 10.3389/fcimb.2019.00454. PMID: 32010640; PMCID: PMC6974441.

Wiertsema SP, van Bergenhenegouwen J, Garssen J, Knippels LMJ. The Interplay between the Gut Microbiome and the Immune System in the Context of Infectious Diseases throughout Life and the Role of Nutrition in Optimizing Treatment Strategies. Nutrients. 2021 Mar 9;13(3):886. doi: 10.3390/nu13030886. PMID: 33803407; PMCID: PMC8001875.

Wu S, Bhat ZF, Gounder RS, Mohamed Ahmed IA, Al-Juhaimi FY, Ding Y, Bekhit AEA. Effect of Dietary Protein and Processing on Gut Microbiota-A Systematic Review. Nutrients. 2022 Jan 20;14(3):453. doi: 10.3390/nu14030453. PMID: 35276812; PMCID: PMC8840478.

Wu X, Wu Y, He L, Wu L, Wang X, Liu Z. Effects of the intestinal microbial metabolite butyrate on the development of colorectal cancer. J Cancer. 2018 Jun 15;9(14):2510-2517. doi: 10.7150/jca.25324. PMID: 30026849; PMCID: PMC6036887.

Yuan X, Chen R, Zhang Y, Lin X, Yang X. Sexual dimorphism of gut microbiota at different pubertal status. Microb Cell Fact. 2020 Jul 28;19(1):152. doi: 10.1186/s12934-020-01412-2. PMID: 32723385; PMCID: PMC7390191.

Zafar H, Saier MH Jr. Gut *Bacteroides* species in health and disease. Gut Microbes. 2021 Jan-Dec;13(1):1-20. doi: 10.1080/19490976.2020.1848158. PMID: 33535896; PMCID: PMC7872030.

Zeb F, Wu X, Chen L, Fatima S, Haq IU, Chen A, Majeed F, Feng Q, Li M. Effect of time-restricted feeding on metabolic risk and circadian rhythm associated with gut microbiome in healthy males. Br J Nutr. 2020 Jun 14;123(11):1216-1226. doi: 10.1017/S0007114519003428. Epub 2020 Jan 6. PMID: 31902372.

Zheng P, Zeng B, Zhou C, Liu M, Fang Z, Xu X, Zeng L, Chen J, Fan S, Du X, Zhang X, Yang D, Yang Y, Meng H, Li W, Melgiri ND, Licinio J, Wei H, Xie P. Gut microbiome remodeling induces depressive-like behaviors through a pathway mediated by the host's metabolism. Mol Psychiatry. 2016 Jun;21(6):786-96. doi: 10.1038/mp.2016.44. Epub 2016 Apr 12. PMID: 27067014.

Zhou X, Willems RJL, Friedrich AW, Rossen JWA, Bathoorn E. Enterococcus faecium: from microbiological insights to practical recommendations for infection control and diagnostics. Antimicrob Resist Infect Control. 2020 Aug 10;9(1):130. doi: 10.1186/s13756-020-00770-1. PMID: 32778149; PMCID: PMC7418317.

Zhao J, Zhang X, Liu H, Brown MA, Qiao S. Dietary Protein and Gut Microbiota Composition and Function. Curr Protein Pept Sci. 2019;20(2):145-154. doi: 10.2174/1389203719666180514145437. PMID: 29756574.